# Blended Family Advice

# Blended Family Advice

A step-by-step guide to help blended and step families become strong and successful

Shirley Cress Dudley, MA LPC

**To order additional copies of this book, contact:**
Xlibris Corporation
1-888-795-4274
www.Xlibris.com
Orders@Xlibris.com
70670

# Contents

## Section Three: Your Ex-Spouse, Parents and the Rest of the World

## Bonus Material

This book is dedicated to my husband Eric
and my blended family, along with
the many blended and step families
who are working hard to create strong and healthy families.

# Endorsements and Reviews of *Blended Family Advice*

"In **Blended Family Advice,** Shirley Cress Dudley lays out a step-by-step game plan for managing a blended family. You will be inspired by the real life success stories included and empowered to take action by the best practices outlined. I would highly recommend parents of teens with blended families read this book and more importantly, put its concepts to practice. Think of it as your blended family owner's manual."

> **Josh Shipp**, Author of *The Teen's Guide to World Domination*, TV Host of Jump Shipp, and Founder of HeyJosh.com

"**Blended Family Advice** is a comprehensive guide to help you live in harmony with your blended family. Shirley Cress Dudley offers you sound advice from learning how to communicate with your new stepchildren, to helping grandparents smoothly adjust to the new family circle. The keys to success in a blended family will be found in this book. **Blended Family Advice** is a quick and easy read, and gives you an action plan to bring your entire family together."

> **Sue Scheff**, Author of *Wit's End* and *Google Bomb*, Founder of Parent's Universal Resource Experts

"An Excellent Book! You can tell from reading **Blended Family Advice** that Shirley Cress Dudley feels passionately about the challenges faced by blended and step families. She offers tested and practical advice to blended families adjusting to their new situation. Most of all, she offers hope based on her personal experience and track record in successfully counseling countless families looking to make the best of their new family."

> **Richard E. Barnes**, Author of *Estate Planning for Blended Families: Providing for Your Spouse & Children in a Second Marriage*

"Shirley Cress Dudley's new book, **Blended Family Advice**, is an excellent resource for parents that are blending their families. Blended families face a myriad of adjustment difficulties and her book provides families with important information to work through these issues. Shirley Cress Dudley's book is truly an invaluable resource for blended families in order to become a cohesive family unit. **Blended Family Advice** is much needed. I will be using it with my blended family clients."

> **Kara T. Tamanini**, M.S., LMHC Psychotherapist, author, and founder of Kids Awareness Series

"Shirley Cress Dudley has nailed this hot topic with her book, **Blended Family Advice**. She taken her first hand experience and honed some real world advice that all blended families should read and heed."

> **Don R. "Dick" Ivey PhD**, Author of *My Marriage was Lousy & My Divorce Ain't So Hot* and *Boiling the Frog—Crises in the American First Family.*

# Preface

Good for you!

You made the decision to invest in your marriage and your blended family. Reading this book and working through the activities, will save you hours of struggles and frustrations in your marriage and your family.

Read it with your spouse and discuss each chapter. You may want to each have your own copy and make notes after each chapter, along with marking the sections you especially want to discuss with your mate.

This book also has optional activities if you'd like to discuss it in a group setting. The group questions may also apply to you as a couple, reading the book together. A group approach, though, will help by providing several other perspectives as you wade through the unfamiliar waters of a newly blended family.

Spend time with the activities and bonus ideas. It is going to be tough, at times, but you can do it!

I wish you and yours a happy, successful blended family!

Sincerely,

Shirley Cress Dudley
MA LPC

# Introduction

Everyday I receive questions from blended and step families. These questions come from Twitter, Linked-in, email, workshops, local counseling and telephone coaching. Although everyone has different questions, many of the issues are very similar. Sometimes I receive the same question from several different families- just different ages or gender of the children and a slightly different scenario.

I started noticing a pattern in the questions. The couples who are having the most difficulties with their blended family are the ones who focus primarily on their kids, ex-spouses, and other areas outside of their marriage. Their questions, at times, focus on how to solve the many conflicts outside of their family, sometimes issues that are beyond their control, and yet are draining a good deal of their time, as they worry about how to solve these issues.

The couples who keep their marriage in the center of the relationship, and the center of the family, mostly have logistical questions, such as how to figure out what kind of house is best for their new family, or how to develop new blended family traditions. These couples, honestly in the minority, aren't struggling with the heart wrenching issues that the majority of families are having difficulty.

Review the two diagrams on the following pages. Compare the differences in The Ideal Blended Family diagram and The Blended Family with Problems diagram. Refer back to these diagrams as we progress through the book and I hope you'll find this visual representation helpful.

# The Ideal Blended Family

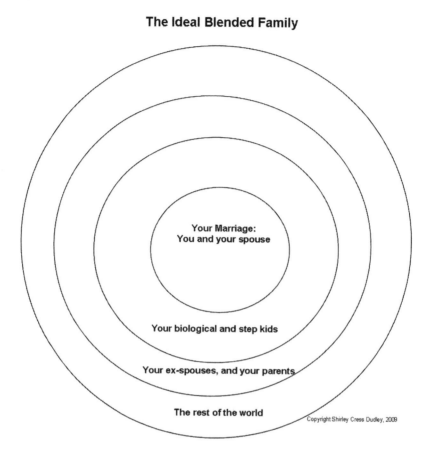

Your Marriage:
You and your spouse

Your biological and step kids

Your ex-spouses, and your parents

The rest of the world

Copyright Shirley Cress Dudley, 2009

Notice that the husband and wife are in the center of the relationship. The kids are outside this circle of marriage, and the ex-spouses, parents and the rest of the world are even farther outside of the marriage circle.

I will refer to this diagram, throughout the book. The majority of the blended and step family issues that occur result in the husband and wife changing their focus and priorities to the outside and away from their marriage.

## Blended Family with Problems

You and your kids

Your spouse and his/her kids

Your Marriage

Ex- spouse and your parents

Ex- spouse and your in-laws

The rest of the world

The second diagram illustrates numerous issues: the marriage of this couple is not a priority. The majority of the couple's time is spent on their kids, ex-spouse and parents, while the marriage (and their blended family) is slowly disappearing. This type of marriage won't succeed long-term, as the husband and wife slowly put more and more energy into areas that cannot be changed (such as bitter, upset ex-spouses, or trying to compensate for the divorce by giving your kids more and more attention and keeping the focus of the family directly on them.) Continue reading, and I'll explain how to keep a healthy balance: love your spouse, your kids, communicate with your ex and the rest of the world, and live, for the most part, happily ever after.

**Couples Activity**

Which of these diagrams best fits your marriage and your family?

List some of the problems in your marriage caused by being part of a blended family:

*

*

*

*

*

List some of the current issues in your blended family:

*

*

*

*

*

Hold on to these lists. As you read the rest of the book, many of these issues will be resolved if you take the steps recommended, in each chapter.

# Section One

# Your Marriage

.

# Chapter One

## It's really tough in the beginning

My family and I have crossed many of the hurdles of blending our family, although we still work to keep ourselves moving along in a cohesive unit. Families aren't perfect, and people aren't perfect. We are in constant need of working to keep relationships strong and healthy. If you haven't been in a blended family, I believe it's impossible to really understand how difficult it is.

I'm a licensed professional counselor, with a master's degree in marriage and family counseling, and another master's degree in education. I've counseled, coached and advised thousands of families on marriage and family issues. With all this training and counseling experience, you would think my blended family would just slide into place, as the perfect family. Well, it didn't! Being a professional in the field of counseling helped, but it was still very tough.

I would like to begin by telling you about the first year in my own blended family. As you read through the book and feel that what I recommend is "too hard" or "won't work" . . . remember, I've been where you are, and we have moved forward. There's hope for your family, too—but it does take a lot of effort and commitment.

Read on, and I'll tell you about my experiences, and also experiences of other families. As you progress through the book, I hope my words will encourage you in your path to being a happy and successful blended family.

## The first year of my blended family

I don't think anyone can really describe the emotions and the pain of blending a family. My fiancé and I were in love, and excited about getting married. Gradually, we exposed our kids to their new step parent—scheduling short meals, fun activities, and talking about the upcoming marriage. There were a few shy smiles, the occasional silent moments, but no major concerns, as we gradually became acquainted with each other. But when the wedding day finally arrived, a couple of the kids, especially one of my new stepdaughters, was NOT happy.

Our wedding photos have some red faces (from crying—and I don't mean happy tears) along with some frowns and a couple of blank stares. I had been divorced for quite some time. My ex and I had divorced almost ten years ago, and he had remarried over five years ago, so my kids were excited about the wedding, having a stepdad and stepsiblings. My husband's situation was different. He had divorced after a 20-year marriage. I was one of the first women he met after he became single. We fell in love and our wedding was scheduled a little less than a year after our first date.

His ex-wife was in a similar situation. She was dating a man and was anticipating an engagement ring in the coming weeks. So, for my new husband's kids, there were many changes, all at once, and they were a bit lost. One of my new stepdaughters were especially upset about the changes. It's hard to emphasize just how upset she felt. She was upset enough to try to destroy our marriage.

She made our life miserable for months-screaming and yelling, removing photos of her father and me and replacing them with photos of her with her father, sabotaging our new house, refusing to participate in family activities, and actually physically pushing me away from her father on several occasions. After her last irrational, physical event, he forbid her to come into our house. He finally set boundaries and guidelines for her, and said that she wasn't welcome until she could abide by his expectations and our house rules, and be polite and civil to everyone when she was in our home.

During the day, he would argue with her on the phone, not allowing her to come over, or participate in any of our family activities. At night, he would lay in bed with me, crying that he couldn't spend time with his daughter. I wanted him to have all of his children with us, but agreed that the aggressive and angry behavior of his daughter was not what we needed in our house as we grew together as a family.

The pain was quite strong and also different among our various family members:

- My husband wanted to have a close relationship with his daughter and yet wanted to continue to blend our new family. He could not tolerate his daughter attacking his new wife, both verbally and physically, and yet wanted a relationship with both his daughter and new wife.
- I wanted to have a relationship with his daughter, but she was very aggressive and angry with me—seeming to blame me for all the changes in her life (although I met her father after he ended his marriage.) Whenever she was in the house, on short, test visits, everyone was on edge, creeping around the house, avoiding her. I wanted my husband happy, and yet—we all seemed happier when this daughter was not present. There didn't seem to be any easy options for us.
- My two biological children hid in their rooms when his daughter was in the house, prisoners in their own homes, not knowing what to do with this angry, new stepsibling. They liked their new stepdad, but didn't understand why he was unhappy all the time.
- My husband's daughter thought she was no longer loved—that her father had replaced her, and that she did not have the same importance to him as before. She saw the marriage as some sort of competition—and I was the enemy. She was confused, angry and very upset at the world that was changing around her.
- My husband's other daughter was confused, wondering if she should side with her sister. Also, if she likes the new stepmom—does that mean she doesn't love her mother anymore? What should she do?

It's so hard to describe this to someone who hasn't experienced it. I hear from so many of you that the negative emotions of blending a family are very overwhelming and quite surprising.

### Where do we go from here?
Let's discuss some of these reactions and figure out where they originate, and how to work through the emotions and feelings. We'll then move towards more positive outcomes.

Thankfully, the strong negative emotions and the gut wrenching pains of my blended family are past. My family is chaotic and busy for the most part, and happy and successful as a family unit. We struggle to coordinate schedules, but the days of yelling, crying, and massive conflicts are over (except when a certain stepdaughter still has an occasional bad day.) Let's figure out what's going on in everyone's head when a new family starts to blend . . .

**The different perspectives: what in the world is everyone thinking?**
I can't cover every possible feeling and every scenario, but here goes . . .

### New stepmom/wife
She is excited about the marriage and her wonderful new husband. She wants the step kids to like her, love her, and think she's great. Although she tries very hard, she's confused when they don't like her, (most step kids don't immediately like their stepmother) and she doesn't know what to do to change their feelings about her.

She loves her biological kids dearly, and wonders if she'll ever love his kids as much as she loves her own. She is a little jealous when her new husband spends a lot of time with his kids, and sometimes even wonders if he loves his kids more than her.

### New stepdad/husband
He is excited about the marriage and his fantastic new wife. He wants to be a great dad to his new step kids and is confused when they don't easily accept him and don't even seem to like him. He loves his wife, but is confused when he spends time with his own kids and she gets upset. He sees his wife spending a lot of time with her kids, and wonders if she loves them more than she loves him. Sometimes he feels she puts her kids in front of his needs. He also sees his kids getting jealous when he spends time with his new step kids. He just doesn't know what to do.

He wants to make everyone happy, but the more time he focuses on his kids—the angrier his new wife becomes. The more he focuses on his wife, the more his kids whine and complain that he is ignoring them. He's confused.

**Stepsiblings**

Younger kids (approximate ages 0-12) accept blended families much more easily and faster than older kids. In their minds, each home should have a mommy and daddy, so it makes sense for their parents to remarry and move in with another adult. They don't really understand why their other biological parent doesn't live with them anymore, but if they can spend time regularly with the noncustodial parent, they are generally content. They will question the divorce as they get older, but right now, it's a little confusing, but seems O.K.

Teenagers (approximate ages 13-19) are not happy with the divorce and remarriage of their parents. They have enough going on in their lives (puberty, hormones, friends, school, and activities) that they are enraged that their mom and dad decided to change their home life. They don't understand why their parent needs to remarry . . . aren't the kids enough to keep you happy? They also see the new spouse as competition, and will watch carefully to see if they are more important, or the new spouse or new kids get more attention.

They are afraid if they like their new stepparent, it means they are disloyal to their biological parent. If they enjoy spending time with a new stepparent, it may even mean that they don't like their biological parent any more. They just don't know how to act, and are pretty mad about the whole situation.

Older kids (ages 20 and up) may no longer live at home and have lives of their own. They are unhappy that their parents divorced, and don't understand why, after all these years, their parents can't get along. They don't see the need to accept this new spouse, and would prefer ignoring the new marriage and just visit mom and dad separately.

**Grandparents**

The parents of the newly married couple may not know *what* to think. They are sad that their adult child has divorced, but they want what's best for him or her. They are happy their adult child has found someone and has remarried. They wonder what is expected of them—at birthdays, holidays and other events, now that there is a new spouse, and new children—ones that aren't related to them.

They wonder why they have to take down the old wedding photos and family photos of their adult child. They are confused and want to do what's best, but really don't know what that may be.

## Summary

In reality, everyone is mainly only thinking from his or her own perspective. They have been thrown together, into a "family"—yet they don't feel like a family. Because of all the new emotions, new experiences, and new family members—it's tough to look outside of yourself and remember that other members of your family are having some confusing times too.

Some of you may be wondering what happened with the angry, aggressive daughter in our blended family. It took us a year of very strong, clear expectations—but she finally figured it all out. She wrote me a letter and asked if we could meet for coffee. I called her and we set the date.

I don't know who was more nervous—her or me. I picked her up and drove us to the closest coffee house I could find. After settling down with our drinks (hot chocolate for me and mocha latte for her,) I told her about my childhood, and how I felt when my parents divorced. I cried as I remembered my confused, angry and sad feelings—and she just listened quietly. I told her that divorce isn't ideal, and that it does leave a hole in your heart, but we have to move on, and make the best of our situations. We then talked about the last year, and she apologized for her behavior. She said she felt as if she lost a year, not getting to know my kids and me. She said she could see that getting married again made her dad happy, and she wants him to be happy.

We agreed to start over . . . start fresh, and let her join our blended family. A week later, we celebrated Christmas with all five of our children present. The one with the largest smile on her face was the stepdaughter who had experienced the roughest year. When it was time for my step kids to gather their presents and other stuff, and head back to their mother's house for her Christmas celebration, she was the one who ran back in to hug me and thank me for a wonderful Christmas.

Precious readers, there is hope. Everyone in your family is confused right now. It's time to figure out what to do, and move forward to creating a cohesive family unit.

Some of you just recently married and have a newly blended family. Some of you have been remarried for years and still haven't figured out how to blend your family into one unit. Starting now . . . right now, it's time to figure it out.

### Couple's Discussion Time

Talk with your spouse about your feelings, fears and hopes. Ask your spouse to share his or her thoughts with you.

### Family Time

Spend some time, alone, with your biological kids, talking about their feelings. If they don't want to talk, read parts of this chapter to them and ask if any of it sounds like their feelings.

Ask your kids—what are your biggest fears about the blended family? Listen to your kids. Don't interrupt or immediately answer them. Here are some common fears you may want to read to your child and ask if any of them fit their fears—

> "My biggest fear is that you'll love your new husband more than you love me."

> "My fear is you'll leave me, like you left my mom."

> "My fear is you'll love your new step kids more than me, since you'll see them more. Maybe you'll even forget me."

Reassure your children that your love for them remains the same and will not change. Remind them that there's no competition between their new stepparents.

**Couple's Time**
Share your child's thoughts with your spouse.

Note: It's O.K. to be honest with each other, as you wade through all these confusing feelings. Negative feelings are acceptable, and should be heard, as long as everyone is respectful of each other's feelings.

**How to survive the first 90 days**
Before we get into the details of how to work through your issues, a few of you may need a basic survival guide, so below is a short primer, *How to survive the first 90 days in a blended family.*

Some of you may believe you can skip this part because you've been married longer than 90 days. Hold on, not just yet. Some of you have been married longer, but your family hasn't progressed much in the blending process. Go ahead and read this next section. If you are doing everything right:

- First—highest praises for you and your family!
- Second—send me your experiences to add to the next edition!
- O.K.—since none of us is perfect (I'm sure not perfect)—read on . . .

### No less love

Remind everyone, at least daily, that there is no less love in a blended family. Everyone who was a valued family member before the "merge" is still a valued family member. Each loved family member is still loved. A blended family provides the opportunity for more love. There are now more people involved, since the marriage, who care about each other and will grow together as a family.

### Strange feelings are O.K.

Your kids did not choose your spouse. You love your new partner, but your children will need some time getting to know this person. It's O.K. if they have some strange feelings, even confusing thoughts—wondering if they are going to like this new stepparent. Let them take their time and get to know your spouse. Remind them to be respectful and friendly, and then give them some space.

### No competitions

A new stepparent does not replace anyone in the family. The children still have their biological parents, with the addition of a new stepparent or two. This stepparent is to be respected as an adult in your home, but does not take the place of either of the biological parents.

There are no competitions. Children sometimes feel that the new stepparent is a new enemy—a competitor for them. The new stepparent may feel competition too and believe that the step kids take time away from their new spouse. Again, remind everyone that there are no competitions and no threats. Relax . . . and get to know each other.

### It's o.k. to like your new stepparent

Sometimes kids believe that liking their stepparent means that they are disloyal to their biological parent. Reassure your child that this is a different relationship, and loving your parents has nothing to do with getting to know and even liking this new stepparent.

### Adults are still in charge

All adults, biological or stepparents, are still the ones in charge. It's best to not keep any secrets from your new spouse. Present yourselves as a "united front" to the kids. If they question you, and you don't have an answer ready (example: a new family rule) tell them that you'll think about it and get back to them. Discuss all issues, in private, with your new spouse. If you and your spouse disagree, do it in private, away from the kids.

### House rules still apply

Some parents believe that the kids have been through so much—the divorce of their parents, remarriage, new homes, etc. that it's time to back down on the discipline. This is not true. Children appreciate structure. Now is not the time to take the structure away, during all of these changes. Be consistent, keep house rules, develop new rules for your new family, and treat all children, biological and step children—the same.

### Keep your marriage at the center of the family

For some of you, the reason your previous marriage failed is because you placed your kids in the center of the relationship. (Refer back to the diagrams in the Introduction.) Remember this mistake and keep you and your spouse in the center of your new family. Set aside time, each day (even if it's just a few minutes at bedtime) to be alone with your spouse. Schedule date nights 2-4 times a month, when the children are not invited, and focus on your marriage. Children thrive in a stable and strong marriage.

You can survive the first 90 days of a blended family. Stay rested, as objective as possible, and keep loving every member of your family!

**Group Discussion**
Introduce yourselves to the group.

- How long have you been remarried?
- What are the ages of your kids?

Discuss how you felt when you read Shirley's experience of her first year. What are the similarities in your family?

What is your reaction after you read about the different perspectives of everyone in a blended family?

# Chapter One Notes

# Chapter Two

## The center of the blended family: you and your spouse

You and your new spouse should be in the center of your blended family. Make sure you schedule time, each day to talk. You may get up early, before the kids are awake, or stay up a little later in the evening to talk. Set aside at least 30 minutes a day to "check in" with your spouse and connect with them.

Date nights are also important. At least once a month, schedule an evening without any kids, and do something enjoyable with your spouse. Focus on your marriage and each other, during these dates. Remember the reasons you married your spouse and celebrate your time together.

Your children are important but should never be the focus of your marriage. You and your spouse should work together to make decisions about your biological and step kids. Your spouse is your first priority. This may be difficult for your children to understand, but many of you have a first failed marriage due to this lack of focus. If children are in the center of the family, the marriage will not last. You are also setting a healthier example for your kids if you focus on the marriage. Blended moms and dads have asked:

> *"But what about my kids? Shouldn't I focus on them? They've been through so much."*

> *"Surely my new spouse knows that a lot of my time will be consumed by my kids."*

*"I want to make sure my kids get what they need and to be the best parent I can be for them."*

*"What if my spouse doesn't care about my kids like I do? How can I know that we'll make the best decisions for my kids?"*

Again, to be the best parent you can be, you need to make your marriage a priority. If you put your marriage first, you and your spouse will do what's best for your family. As we walk through the various issues blended and step families face, remember the two diagrams of an *Ideal Blended Family* and *A Blended Family with Issues*. You will find that focusing on your marriage and putting your spouse first will solve many of your issues. I will continue to focus on this point throughout the rest of the book. Read on and it will make more sense to you.

**Group Discussion**

Refer back to the diagrams in the front of the book. Which of these diagrams best fits right now?

Which of these diagrams fits your first marriage?

Discuss some issues you and your spouse are having difficulty resolving. Share with the group, if you are comfortable.

\*

\*

\*

\*

\*

# Chapter Two Notes

# Chapter Three

## Developing great communication skills

Do you ever feel like your spouse is talking, going on and on and on, about the same topic? Yes? Well, sometimes we continue to talk when we feel that the other person does not understand us or isn't listening. Below are a few tips that will improve your communication skills and help your spouse feel listened to and understood.

It's important to work on communication skills, now more than ever. Communication is one of the primary reasons marriages fail. You will need these skills to have a successful marriage with your new spouse.

### Honesty and clarity

Honesty and clarity are essential ingredients to great communication. Think through what is important to you and discuss calmly those needs with your new spouse. If some issues are very emotional for you, you may want to write them down first.

### Use "I" statements

Use "I" statements—not "You" statements. This reduces tension with your spouse and creates a sense of responsibility and ownership of your topic as you speak.

Make decisions and discuss important topics in private, with only you and your spouse present.

**Hints:**

- Do not discuss important topics in front of the kids
- Do not argue in front of the kids—always present a united front

## Let me think about it

It's always O.K. to tell the kids, "Let me think about it" if they ask for something and you and your spouse disagree. An immediate answer is not always necessary. You can also come up with a cue or special phrase to use with your spouse, to let them know you want to discuss an issue further. Figure out a phrase or an action that you can do or say, in public, that has meaning only to you and your spouse. This phrase or action will signify the need to explore a topic later.

## Huh?

Take turns talking. Listen carefully while your spouse is talking. Nod your head and comment, as he or she talks—to communicate your understanding. When it's your turn, your spouse should do the same. Do not interrupt, unless you are asking a clarifying question. When your spouse is finished sharing—paraphrase by saying back what you thought you heard. Ask your spouse if your understanding is correct. You will find that if your spouse feels understood, communication will be more successful and productive.

Sometimes your spouse will understand you, but not agree with you. Decide if this issue is one of the important ones. If so—tell your spouse. If this is not an important issue, this may be one to compromise and let your spouse have their way. Remember that both of you came from different backgrounds and have varied experiences. If you can't agree, find a way for both of you to compromise a little, and yet come to a unifying decision.

## Couple's Activity

If you have a great deal of emotion over a particular topic, write that topic down and set aside a time for you and your spouse to discuss it. List a few topics you want to discuss with your spouse.

Before you begin this topic, tell your spouse 3 things you appreciate about them. Encourage them to share 3 things they appreciate about you.

After this activity—tell them that you have an issue to discuss, and it's quite important to you, so you have written it down. Read the issue to your spouse (or let them read it silently.) Now quietly and calmly, begin discussing possible solutions.

### Group Discussion

Bring your notes from your couple's time at home and read to the group three things you appreciate about your spouse.

*His Notes*                                    *Her Notes*

\*                                             \*


\*                                             \*


\*                                             \*


Share some of the issues you and your spouse are currently working through. Discuss how each of you can compromise to reach a decision on these issues.

# Chapter Three Notes

# Chapter Four

## Financial discussions

### Set priorities

If you have been single for a while, you are used to making decisions on your own. Now that you've remarried, another adult expects to be a part of those decisions, and you should be prepared to discuss *any* major financial decision with your spouse.

It's crucial to your marriage to be honest. Discuss your goals and dreams. Spend some time deciding what your financial priorities are for the next 12 months, 5 years and 10 years. Talk through these priorities with your spouse. Some of your priorities may be very different, but that's O.K. Develop a list that both of you can agree on, and plan your budget around these goals.

### Free money

Choose an amount of "free" money that each of you can spend each week. This amount does not need to be accounted for. This may be for lunches, small purchases, etc. The two of you are the only ones who can decide what amount is fair. Choose this amount and STICK TO IT! No purchases over this amount are allowed (unless you decide it's O.K.) without discussing the purchase, in advance, with your spouse.

Have you heard the story about the young husband who went to the store for diapers and came home with a Wii entertainment system? Or the wife that went out for a pair of tennis shoes and came back with a pair of diamond earrings? These are the horror stories of couples that didn't decide on a sum each could spend, each week, without any questions, accountability or discussion. Make it a priority, this week, to decide on your amount of weekly unaccounted or free money.

## Children's allowance

Giving children an allowance teaches them how to value money. Guide your children to save 10% and give/donate 10% of each week's allowance. This teaches good money management, delayed gratification, and responsibility. For the younger ones, piggy banks with the different sections (save, give, spend) are available on the internet.

An allowance also keeps each child from regularly asking for money. Assign each child several daily and weekly family chores, and compensate your children for their work. As children grow into teenage years, increase responsibilities and chores along with the allowance, and this money becomes their entertainment fund.

## Create a budget

Create a spreadsheet that will assist you in planning your family budget. There are many examples, on the internet; several of which are free.

*You will want to include:*

- Your incomes
- Child support (as income or an expense)
- Utilities (gas, water, electricity, cable, internet, telephone and cell phones)
- Mortgage or Rent
- Home or Renter's insurance
- Groceries and household supplies
- Auto insurance
- Car payment(s)
- Auto expenses: gas, repairs/maintenance
- Insurance: Health, dental, vision, life
- Education: tuition, childcare expenses
- Entertainment: movies, plays, dining out, travel
- Children's allowances and other children's expenses
- Savings each month: savings account, retirement account)
- Donations
- Miscellaneous (anything else you can think of that is a monthly expense)

## Don't forget an updated last will and testament

This may be a topic you aren't comfortable discussing, but it is crucial in your newly blended family. You and your spouse need to immediately consider estate planning. You may have this all taken care of in your first marriage, but now things are very different. Your current will is inaccurate and should be updated.

It's a little more complicated in a blended family. (You can't just mark out your old spouse's name and insert the new one!) If one of you dies, you don't want the entire estate to go to your new spouse; you want to make arrangements to also provide for your children.

Talk with your spouse and figure out your goals. Do you need to provide for underage children's education? What if one of you becomes disabled? Identify your financial and family concerns.

Don't forget discussions about end-of-life decisions. There are many professionals available that specialize in estate planning. You can now find professionals that specialize in blended family estate planning, if you search your phone book and the internet.

Some people are afraid of talking about death and estate planning. If you will spend some time with your spouse, and then a trained attorney, this is a task you can complete and have a wonderful feeling of accomplishment, knowing you have provided for your family.

### Question:
*"Should we have separate or joint accounts?"*
There are no right answers to this question except that you should have whatever the two of you both believe is fair. With child support issues, sometimes separate accounts are helpful. Whatever the two of you . decide is best, as long as your spouse is informed. Honesty is the best way to run your household finances, and will keep your marriage intact.

### Couple's Activity
Read the Bonus Report: **Financial Planner for the Blended Family**
Do the activities and the discussions.

**Group Discussion**

Share with the group, what is the amount of "free money" in your family and why?

Have you updated your will?

What local attorney would you recommend to update your will that is a blended family expert?

How do you feel about giving your kids an allowance related to their chores? If you disagree, discuss with the group what your solution is to teaching responsibility in the family. Discuss the pros and cons of each approach.

Share with the group if you and your spouse developed your own Excel spreadsheet. Share with the group a budget spread sheet you found on the internet that works for your family. (Bring the website address to your meeting.)

What budget areas are you and your spouse having difficulties making decisions on what's best for your family?

# Chapter Four Notes

# Section Two

# Your Kids—
# Biological and Step

# Chapter Five

## Parenting

### How do we handle the kids?

You're married and one or both of you brought children into the new marriage. You need to come to an understanding on parenting and discipline that feels fair to both of you.

It's important to respect the biological parent's history of parenting, but still come to a mutual understanding of how *all children* will be treated and disciplined in your home. It's time for the two of you to discuss boundaries and guidelines for your kids and your home.

#### Couple's Activity

Plan an evening, alone with your spouse, to decide what's really important. Agree on house rules and guidelines for your newly blended home. Figure out a time to explain these guidelines to your children. A wonderful opportunity to have a family meeting is soon after you've moved into a new home, or when the new spouse arrives with her kids into an existing home. Make sure all children are present. Present the new guidelines together, as a couple. You will need a separate notebook to create and keep these guidelines and house rules. A few spaces in this book will not be adequate. You will also need to leave room for negotiations and compromise, as you two work through your suggested house rules and guidelines.

**All kids should be treated fairly and equally.**
All of your children, whether biological or step, should be treated fairly and equally. You and your spouse can create house rules such as:

- No eating in the living room
- No T.V. after 9pm on a school night
- Everyone helps clean up the kitchen after meals
- Each person keeps his or her room clean and bed made

These rules will apply to every child in your family. Consequences can be different, based on age differences and developmental stage, but consequences need to be equal and fair.

Note: it also helps if the adults follow the same rules. It's hard to explain why Dad is eating in the living room, and no one else can!

This is your new home and your blended family. Create house rules and guidelines that will give your children boundaries and direction. Your children will function better in an environment in which they understand what is expected of them. Your children will also be watching carefully to see if the biological children are treated differently than the stepchildren. Be very careful with your words and actions, as the children are watching to see if you really mean what you say.

**Biological parent takes the lead**
The biological parent should always take the lead in the discipline of their kids. The new stepparent should not be perceived as the "heavy," or the one who is the enforcer of the rules.

If your child disobeys a house rule—deal with the issue, immediately, with your spouse at your side. The children should always see you two as a united front—even if you don't agree on everything—appear united to them, and work out the differences in private, later.

**Be consistent**
If you make a rule—keep it, everyday. Don't change the rules on the days you are tired, or the days your spouse is out of the house or out of town.

**No secret alliances with your biological kids**

If you change the rules when your spouse is not at home, this causes your children to not respect their stepparent, and believe that the bond between you and them is stronger than the bond between you and your spouse. Your relationship with your spouse should take priority. Keeping your relationship strong with your spouse provides a stable and consistent environment for your children. This stability and consistency will create feelings of security for your children and will move your blended family to a strong, successful and united family.

*Question*

*"What if my spouse and I disagree on our methods of parenting?"*

There is a very good chance that you and your spouse will disagree on several issues. Decide which issues are very important to you and explain to your spouse why you parent in this way.

There will be some issues that are not as important to you as others are. I suggest these topics may be the ones to compromise with your spouse. All rules should apply to all children. Your kids are going to look for consistency and fairness in your new blended family.

It's not possible to have two distinctly different styles of parenting in one home without creating havoc among the other children.

*Question*

*"My spouse doesn't believe in any type of discipline and lets the kids do anything they want—help!"*

Your spouse should be reading along, in this book with you, talking through the ideas, and working through the activities. So—hopefully after your spouse reads this material, some progress will be made.

Children arrive into this world with parents, not on their own—they don't come equipped with the capability to make decisions on their own. It's our duty, as parents and adults, to give them guidelines and boundaries. If we didn't, there could be some funny consequences:

your children running around naked like wild banshees, eating candy all day and chasing the mail carrier like dogs!

Is this example too radical for you to imagine? Well, imagine the young woman who was never told "no" by her parents, responding to a dress code at her new job by refusing to dress appropriately. This young woman, no matter how bright she is, will be out of a job soon.

Imagine the young man who has never had any boundaries or guidelines. He is speeding down the street, running red lights, ignoring all traffic rules. If he doesn't kill someone or himself, he will end up with a stack of tickets and probably time in jail when he argues with the police officer.

Our *duty* as parents is to give our children guidance, boundaries and discipline. Discipline? Yes—that sounds tough and it is. It is tough to tell a child no, and as your child grows older, it is also helpful (but difficult for you) to let your kids experience the natural consequences of their poor choices and decisions. Parenting our children shows them our love.

It's our *responsibility* as loving parents to discipline, teach, and give guidelines to our children. Here are some additional questions I have received from blended families.

### Question

*"My kids have been through so much—my divorce and now my new marriage. Shouldn't I just give them a break and loosen up on my discipline?"*

This is an example of a parent experiencing guilt. No, your discipline should remain the same:

- Your values haven't changed and you should continue to teach your children the difference between right and wrong
- Boundaries and guidelines show your children that you love them
- Providing discipline actually gives the consistency and security your kids need in a time when a lot of things are changing around them

### Question

*"My step kids spend every other weekend with us and a few weeks of the summer. My husband spends every moment with them when they are here. He's always nervous, and wanting to make each weekend perfect. I feel that he is ignoring me on these weekends and putting his kids first. What can I do?"*

This is another example of a parent experiencing guilt over their divorce and remarriage, and this parent is trying to compensate for their children's loss. Your question is very common, and sometimes I hear this issue 3-5 times a week from other blended families.

This marriage won't be successful until the husband and wife focus on their marriage, not the kids. After talking with this mom, I was told that her husband feels guilty about the divorce and his remarriage and feels he owes it to his kids to give them dedicated time on their weekend visits. Although I understand his concerns, he is not setting a good example of a healthy marriage for his children. If the children are put in the center of the marriage, and are the focus of the family, the marriage will suffer and there won't be a family. His kids will also follow his example and will one day marry and raise their children in this same dysfunctional manner.

The husband needs to guide his children into accepting the new reality—he's remarried and they are now part of a stepfamily. He can convey his expectations for the time spent in his home and with their blended family. Children who visit their noncustodial parent need to be integrated into the family on their weekend visits, not taken away on special outings—dedicated to just pleasing the kids. The children will actually enjoy being a part of the blended family as time progresses. Kids don't know what to do or what expectations we have of them until we teach them. Its fine to take your biological children out for errands, or an occasional special activity—but your focus should be on your marriage and blending the family as a whole.

Look for a balance. Weekends with the noncustodial kids should contain three components: blended family time, parent/child dedicated time and couple's time.

### *Question*

*"We are a blended family. My 17-year-old daughter and I moved into my husband's house and he has a 19-year-old daughter at home. She rarely does any chores and her dad does not make her do any. I buy the groceries and clean up. I make my 17-year-old help me clean. My husband does not understand why this bothers me so much. How can I get my husband to understand this is not right?"*

There are several issues:

- Your stepdaughter sees you as an invasion to her home. You want to change the rules, but she doesn't see the need to change. She has probably acted this way for some time (and it probably worsened when her parents divorced) and wonders why a new person (you) wants her to change her behavior.
- Your children (biological and step) are being treated differently.
- You and your husband have not established your new blended home yet.

It sounds as it moving into a new home isn't an option. In this economy, I truly understand. If that were possible, I would recommend it as the ideal scenario. All family members start fresh with a new home and new house rules and expectations. However—in your current situation, it's time for you and your husband to establish yourselves as the new parental unit of the home. This means that you are establishing your new blended home—one that comes with new house rules and expectations.

Spend some quality time with your husband, explaining how this is your home too, and you would like to figure out ways everyone in the family feels like this is home, and everyone is treated as an equal family member.

Take some time and talk with him about how you imagine the house to function, and how you see each family member participating. Use "I" words, not "you." Don't focus on your stepdaughter's issues; instead, concentrate on the way you imagine things could be. For example, "I imagine a household where everyone picks up after themselves, everyone has assigned chores, and we all work together as a family."

Discuss with your husband what house rules and expectations you believe are important. Make a list of guidelines for your teenage girls to follow. Make sure you both agree, before you present these ideas to the girls. Each of you may have to compromise to get what's most important to you, but the idea is to develop your own house rules, for this family. When you talk with the girls, you need to appear as united. Any indecision or changes to these guidelines should be made between the two of you, without the girls present.

Tell the girls that you are going to have a family meeting, and make sure they are both present. Explain to both girls that, with the new blended marriage, you want this to be home for all of us. You want to treat all siblings fairly, and also make this a happy and functioning home for everyone. Take turns talking, so that both of you are sharing the new guidelines with the girls.

Designate responsibilities for each teenager. These responsibilities come with living in the home and acting as a family member. Responsibilities may include doing the dishes, cleaning the house and helping to prepare meals. There should also be a list of personal duties related to cleaning up after yourself, keeping your room and areas clean, etc.

Remind both girls that you love them and want what's best for them. As long as they live with you, they are under your care and your supervision. As they get older and more independent (which the 19 year old should be heading in this direction, if she is not in school,) they will eventually want to move out on their own, and make their own decisions. But, as long as they live with you, they will be under your guidelines and expectations.

There should also be consequences for not doing your part as a family member. Any child (no matter what age) that is still living in the home should follow parent's instructions. You may need to take away use of a phone, car, or television until you see your guidelines met. Make sure your husband takes the lead in enforcing rules with his daughter, and your take the lead with your daughter.

It may be difficult, at first, for your husband to enforce rules and guidelines with his daughter, if things have gotten a little lax over the last couple of years. It is the responsibility of a parent to do what's best for our children. This includes giving them life skills, consequences and guidance to be successful in this world. Discipline is difficult, but as long as the child is in your care (i.e. living in your home, eating your food, and you are paying some of their bills,) it is still your responsibility to guide this child in the best way you can.

It's going to be tough at first; I'm sure the changes will be hard for your stepdaughter and for your husband, but these changes are good. Remind your husband why you love him, why you married him, and how much you love being married to him. Work together, as a couple to make this house a home for all of your blended family.

### Question
*"My ex-spouse and I never agreed on house rules for our kids. She didn't believe in discipline and thought our kids should be able to do whatever they wanted to do. What do I do now that the kids are visiting my house every other weekend?"*

First, I'm very sorry you had this experience. You are now reaping the negative consequences of raising kids without boundaries and discipline. I imagine your blended home is having quite a lot of issues. There's always a chance to change your parenting style (if your kids are still in the home, and even if they only visit every other week.) Your children want your praise. You can still have a great deal of influence over your kids, even if you only see them a couple of times a month. Tell your kids that you have remarried and there are new rules and guidelines for this home. Explain that you know it's different, but this is what you want, and you intend to enforce the new guidelines and expectations.

### Question
*"I married a man that had no children. We have 2 kids together and I also have 2 children from another marriage. My teenage daughter is*

*always fighting with my husband. He is upset if I don't take his side, and she is upset if I don't stick up for her. What can I do?"*

I understand you are in a difficult situation. You feel in the middle, between your husband and your daughter—wanting to defend/protect/support both of them. Let's back away from the issues and start over a bit.

It's time for you and your husband to create blended family rules and guidelines for your family. These guidelines will apply to everyone in the house (biological kids, step kids—everyone.) You and your husband will develop these house rules and guidelines in your couple's time—with only the two of you present. Make sure each of you expresses your needs and goals for the family. You both may need to compromise a little, but be prepared to present these guidelines to the kids together as a married couple.

If the kids do not follow your guidelines, make sure they know there will be consequences. Consequences should be fair for all kids, although maybe a little different based on their developmental stages. Examples: time out for the little ones, younger teens lose their phones, and older teens lose use of the car for a set period of time.

Let the biological parent be the "heavy" in enforcing the rules for the kids. The stepparent should be in a supportive role, but not the lead role in the discipline. This should work if you both agree on the guidelines, remind the kids, and then enforce consequences.

You and your husband are the center of the marriage. Making guidelines is crucial to the stability of your home. You are not favoring one person over another by forming guidelines—you are parenting your kids in the best way you can. Remind all kids that you love them and expect kindness and respect in your home. The adults should set the example.

**Conclusion**
Some of you are shaking your heads, and believing this is all too difficult to accomplish. Trust me, I truly do understand. It *is* possible to make a difference—even now. My biological kids were raised by me (a marriage

and family counselor and educator,) and their daddy (a former minister,) so they had strict rules and boundaries from birth.  My husband's family was very different. One of my step daugther's told me that, "My mom let's us do whatever we want, and never tells us what to do."

When I brought up the subject of house rules, my husband was happy that we agreed on setting boundaries for our kids, but wondered if his children could make the necessary changes. We decided that our home would be different, and mutually agreed upon guidelines and expectations for our home.

It did take a while, and more than a few negative consequences; but all of our kids understand that the rules in our house our different from their other parent's house. They follow our house guidelines, ask for permission to do activities, and experience consequences when they do not follow our family rules. Good parenting will always prevail. It's the right thing to do, and it's our responsibility as parents.

I've overheard my youngest stepdaughter admonish her older brother (home from college) when he doesn't put his dirty dishes in the dishwasher. Although she is the youngest, she visits more often than her siblings, and is the most positive example for her older brother and sister.

We had some pretty serious issues to work through when our blended family was new. You remember the experience we had with one of my husband's daughters during our first year. She believed if she protested enough, yelled and screamed, and caused enough havoc, we would find it easier to end our marriage and let her dad go back to being single, or maybe even remarry her mother. She discovered, after a year of very strong boundaries and repeated expectations from us, that a united parental front is very hard to sabotage and destroy. When her mother remarried, we believe the ground rules and expectations we set for our blended family helped her transition into her second blended family. Now, no matter which house she visits when home from college, there is a stepparent and several stepsiblings living there. It's a definite change in her world, but one she is getting used to and accepting as her new reality.

You can make a difference in your home. Focus your efforts on your spouse: agreeing on house rules and guidelines, communicating these expectations to your kids, and enforcing consequences for their disobedience. Or . . . you can have children running around like wild animals, yelling at you and attempting to run your home . . .your choice. Remember, I've been there. I know it's difficult to discipline your kids, at times, but it's much easier than experiencing the consequences of an undisciplined house.

One of the most frequent issues I hear from blended families is related to differences in discipline. Invest time with your spouse in developing mutually agreed upon house rules and guidelines for your family. The time spent will save you hours of discomfort.

### Bonus Activity
This is for those of you that have trouble disciplining . . .
Your child has disobeyed a house rule. Take the child to a separate room and explain they have violated a house rule and will experience consequences.

Ask your child for a list of consequences that they believe is fair for this disobedience. (You will be surprised at how honest children are in giving good ideas.) Take this list, and add a few of your own. Choose from this list and remind your child that the consequences will increase the next time. Here is a place to make notes from this experience:

### Other issues in parenting:
### The myth of the wicked stepmother
Unfortunately, our children have been brought up on Disney movies that tell of the wicked stepmother. It's rare for a child to immediately accept and like his stepmother. It's very easy for children to feel like the victim in the new marriage and take out all of their negative emotions on the new stepparent. Here's a humorous look at a *real* wicked stepmother.

1. **You ask your husband to choose between you and his kids**
   You see the kids as competition and you're determined to win.

2. **You don't know much about your step kids**
   You spend all of your time focusing on your own kids and your new husband and don't see the need to get to know your step kids

3. **You ask your husband to take *you* out to dinner on his child's birthday, and tell him to celebrate the kid's birthday on another day.**

4. **You don't recognize the stepchildren's birthdays or any other special events in their lives.**

5. **You treat your kids better than his kids**
   You make sure your children have everything that they need and let their biological mom figure out what her own kid's need.

6. **You interrupt your husband when he's on the phone with his kids**
   What could he possibly be talking about that's more important than you?

7. **You let his kids figure out on their own, where to sleep, and put their stuff, when they visit their Dad.**
   After all, the beds in the house are for the ones who live here full time, right?

8. **You have different house rules for your kids then for his kids.**

9. **You don't let your step kids bring friends into your house.**

10. **You don't let your step children spend any time alone with their Dad when they come to visit.**

All kidding aside, being a stepmom (or stepdad) is one of the toughest jobs in the world. When you marry a man with kids, you commit to love and care for his kids as if they were your own. The kids don't usually appreciate a new stepparent and will not appreciate your efforts for some time (sometimes they never acknowledge the positive impact you have had on their lives.)

Stepparents are not in competition with the kids, although many people feel that way. Although you want to spend time as a blended family, it's a good idea to give your husband some individual time with his children, when they come to visit. Spend this time with your kids, or doing something for yourself. Your step kids will appreciate this time and also feel more comfortable with the blended family time.

### Group Discussion
Did you find any reasons for your kids to call you a wicked stepparent?

How hard is it to think of parenting from your step kid's perspective?

Share some house rules that you have developed in your blended family.

*

*

*

*

*

*

*

*

*

*

Write down some additional house rules or ideas you hear in the group, to be discussed later with your spouse.

*

*

*

*

*

*

# Chapter Five Notes

# Chapter Six

## Creating a sense of unity in your newly blended family

You have remarried and blended a group of people. Except for you and your spouse, no one else chose to be in this group—so there may be a little resistance in making this one big, happy family.

Express to your children how new this all is, and how we will work together, to make this newly blended group feel like family. Remind them to treat others in the family as they would like to be treated, and remember that this is hard for everyone, as we get to know each other. Tell them that you are happy in your new marriage and want to have a strong blended family.

Plan informal, fun activities that will bond your family. These activities don't have to be elaborate vacations or expensive trips to the theme park, but can be simple, planned activities at home. Look at the developmental stages of your children and plan appropriate activities to their age. You are creating memories by planning activities that they can do together. Don't worry if one of your activities doesn't turn out as you planned. I think one of our more interesting ideas was when my company gave us free tickets to see a Neil Diamond concert. Two of our teenage girls bonded over how boring the concert was! Another blended family told me that their most memorable holiday meal was when the turkey fell on the floor and was ruined! Your days don't need to be perfect to make a memory for your blended family.

Make sure everyone participates in your family activity, no matter how simple it is. If you are cleaning up after dinner, make sure everyone has a task to help with the clean up. Tell them everyone needs to participate, as a family member, and none of the kids is a guest. As you do these tasks, continue to use words, such as "we" and "family" that remind your kids that this group is now a new family.

Its O.K. to spend some time alone with just your children, but don't schedule it at a time that inconveniences the rest of the family. Make sure that each time the visiting children are here, there is at least one planned activity for the entire group.

## Plan fun activities at home
Schedule informal, fun activities for family members. Plan events around the holidays—such as decorating the house, dying Easter eggs, and carving pumpkins. Family meals are also a good time to get to know each other with cookie decorating, fondue dipping, and grilling out. Even washing the cars together (with a little unrestricted hose squirting) can be fun.

## Plan interesting outings and vacations
Summer is coming and you and your new spouse are wondering . . .

What should we do? Do you have the fantastic idea of taking your newly blended family on a 3-week car ride all around the United States? Uh Oh . . . maybe you haven't thought this through.

Your spouse is asking if maybe we should just take separate vacations. Nope—that's not the answer either!

## Keep it simple
So—it is *really* wrong to take a 3-week car ride all over the United States? No, not really. If your blended family has been together for over a year or two, the kids are small, or you have a large recreational vehicle—then it sounds like a wonderful adventure. But, if you're just starting out, I don't recommend it. That's too close quarters and a lot of patience for adults and children to have for such a long amount of time.

I remember traveling in the back of my father's grey Chevrolet Impala. My mother and father sat in the front seats—and my sister, grandmother, and I sat in the back—with my grandmother in the middle to prevent fights! We traveled for three weeks, all over the United States—staying in hotels without air conditioning and piling two kids and a grandmother into one queen or sometimes even a double bed.

We stopped when we were tired and saw the lights of the next available hotel on the road. (I really don't recommend this capricious way of vacationing!) But—we saw quite a few national landmarks, such as the Corn Palace, Mount Rushmore, Carlsbad Caverns and the Golden Gate Bridge. We ate lots of fun foods, and had an amazing adventure. Planning adventures such as this for your new family are great, but just wait a few years until they get used to each other!

**Keep it fair**

Taking vacations separately is not *completely* wrong either, just a little difficult. When families blend in a new marriage, the kids are watching to see if everyone is going to be treated the same. The kids initially expect to receive special treatment from their biological parent, but this sort of behavior just leads to parental conflicts and a sense of instability, insecurity and uncertainty in your household. Keep it completely fair, among all kids at all times. Also, make sure the kids view their parent and step parent as one cohesive unit.

If there are vacation issues in which you and your spouse disagree, move this discussion to a private place—away from the kids. Don't reappear until your issues are resolved and you can stand together to discuss your future vacation plans.

I only recommend separate vacations under certain circumstances:

- The school breaks are different (i.e. spring break) and the kids are out at different times. Take each group of kids on similar vacations, but at different times.
- You want to take one child on a vacation, alone, to celebrate an accomplishment (i.e. graduation from high school or college.) This type of trip is fine, but remember that the other kids expect to be given a trip just like their sibling or stepsibling!

We gave my daughter a 2-night trip to the mountains for high school graduation. My daughter and a female buddy chose the location and planned all the activities themselves. Now her brother (only a sophomore in high school) is anxiously awaiting his trip, and already planning *his* two-night graduation trip!

## Keep it short
The best initial vacations for a newly blended family are weekend getaways—not more than 3-4 nights. These are trial adventures, for your family to get to know each other. Examples of these types of trips:

- Weekend in the mountains
- Weekend at the beach
- Weekend at a historical city/location
- 3-4 night cruise

## Planning the trip
Let your kids take part in trip planning. Give them choices and vote on the most popular vacation choice. Of course, you and your spouse have the final decision, and you both should have spent some time alone, developing and discussing options before presenting the choices to your children.

Have each child, based on their developmental stages—research the locations and figure out what fun activities are available at your chosen vacation site. While traveling, have kids take turns navigating and helping the driver make the necessary turns. When someone asks, "Are we there yet?" assign the navigator the responsibility of giving the response of how much longer.

### Weekend in the mountains
This is a great, inexpensive way to get away and create some wonderful memories. Ideas for a trip to the mountains include day hikes, driving and looking at the autumn leaves and scenic views, exploring a cave, and going horseback riding.

Focus on the outdoors and enjoy the time with nature. Children naturally love to be outside. Take advantage of this and enjoy the wonderful weather and the beautiful scenery. Taste the local cuisine, apple cider, boiled peanuts, and homemade jams.

Here's one blended family's experience . . .

*"We took our blended family, ages 8-18, on a weekend trip to the North Carolina Mountains. We decided to spend the first day at Tweetsie Railroad (and old cowboy themed park) and received a few grunts and folded shoulders from our older kids—ages 16 and 18. But after riding a few rides, watching the pretend gunfights, eating tons of junk food, and taking lots of silly photos—all of our kids were smiling.*

*The next day we went horseback riding. It was quite funny, because the younger kids had ridden horses before, and the teenagers had never . been on a horse. All of the kids had fun galloping (slowly) through the meadows, and following the beautiful mountain trails. That night, we laughed and told stories during dinner, and finished up with a family swim in the hotel pool, with stepsiblings splashing water and playing together. It was quite a successful weekend and we all had fun."*

**Weekend at the beach**
Walking on the beach and hearing the waves hit the shore is very relaxing and soothing. Some of your family may be sunbathers (don't forget the sunscreen!) and some may be shoppers. You may also have the go-kart and amusement park enthusiast. Try to tailor your trip to meet all of the family's varied interests, along with the daily weather report.

Have a puzzle or some board games available in the hotel room in case you have a couple of rainy days in a row. Shopping and also renting movies are other ideas for the cooler or wet days.

This isn't time to visit the outer banks or a lonely island. Make sure you find a beach that offers activities for all of your family. Mix up activities, based on the weather and the interests of your group.

**Weekend at a historical location**
This is a great opportunity to learn a little about history. Do some research in advance, to prepare the kids for the trip. Take into consideration the developmental stages of your kids and their attention spans. Trips to the museum are great, but don't make it the entire trip. Several historical locations also have attractions for

kids. Ask your kids which activities they are interested in, and plan various excursions during your weekend visit.

### 3-4 night cruise

Cruises offer activities for all ages and are really reasonably priced. Watch for specials in the newspaper, and also check the internet rates. Usually your local travel agent will match any rate you can find on the internet. There are many different cruise lines for you to choose from.

Cruises offer non-stop activities for all ages; with babysitting services for the tiny ones, camp for the younger kids, and even teen activities and parties for the older kids. Cruise lines have become very creative and even offer rock climbing and mini-golf courses on the ship. Cruise lines take every opportunity to make the trip safe and enjoyable for all ages. The benefit of a cruise is that all ages will have choices throughout the day. You can meet up for lunch and dinner while everyone heads their separate ways during the day.

The rooms are very small, but you spend very little time, except sleeping, in the cabins. Spending extra money on a larger cabin is usually a waste of money. There is unlimited food, 24 hours a day, from hamburgers to filet mignon.

Choose a port close to your home. This will cut down on your cost if you can drive to the port, instead of taking an airplane. Cruise lines also offer discounts on airfare if you purchase them at the same time as the cruise. Discounts are offered on the third and fourth persons in each cabin, and bunk beds are common.

The all-inclusive price of a cruise can lower your vacation budget—if you skip the port tours (which charge extra fees.) Your kids will have the opportunity to be with their stepfamily and also have supervised freedom (you can't get off the ship!) during your vacation.

### Keys to success

You don't always have to stay together, the entire weekend as a blended family. Mix it up a bit. Your children will be watching to see if anyone gets any special treatment. Let older teenagers take younger children on a short outing, while the adults have some time alone. Split up with your biological children for a couple of hours, but make sure you do similar or equal activities. Or, husband takes the boys and wife takes the girls on separate outings. Anyway you divide the group, just keep in mind that fairness needs to prevail.

## Keep a record of the event

Take informal, candid photos of your group. Every now and then, when things are going well, take some group shots. The kids may frown at first, but once they get used to your new camera addiction, you will be greeted with smiles and some silliness, when you pull out your camera.

Once your arrive home, and have finished washing the mounds of clothes, put these photos in a family album or scrapbook. Let interested kids assist in writing captions for the photos. Little ones can recite their favorite memories and you can put them in the scrapbook. Label this album, "Our Family." Add more photos, regularly to this album, as your family continues to celebrate fun events and make more trips.

Frame your favorite photos and put them on the wall or in a heavily trafficked room for all to see and remember. You are declaring to the world that you are a family, and you're proud of it!

### Question
*"What do we do about the room arrangements?"*

With families, you want to be comfortable and yet cost efficient. Divide children up by gender, in the bedrooms. It doesn't make sense to put a boy and girl sibling in a room together when a boy and girl stepsiblings are next door.

If possible, and your children are at least 12 years old, it would be nice to have adjoining rooms, with you and your new spouse in your own room. Avoid the temptation to have a "your family" and "my family" separate rooms—this perpetuates the theme that you are two separate families.

### Question
*"My spouse's teenagers sometimes dress inappropriately. With our upcoming trip to the beach, I'm a little worried. What can I do?"*

This is not a vacation issue; this is a parenting issue. You and your spouse need to re-discuss your house rules and expectations of all children. If you both disapprove of some of the apparel choices of one of your teenagers, you need to state clearly to this teenager, what the expectations of this household are and that she will need to dress appropriately, when visiting.

Vacation is not a time to test these boundaries. Make sure your expectations are stated and enforced, long before the kids start packing clothes for the trip. The biological spouse should take the lead in the discipline and reminding kids of the boundaries and guidelines.

### Question
*"My ex is going to take my kids on an expensive vacation. How can I compete with this?"*

You will discover that kids don't value the money you spend, they value the time you spend with them. Don't worry about competing with your ex. You and your new spouse should choose vacations and outings that fit your budget. Your children will have just as wonderful memories camping out by the lake, telling stories to Dad in the dark, as they will sitting by the pool of a luxurious hotel, drinking soft drinks with Mom.

**Another blended family vacation experience:**
*"We took our six-year-old boys (one mine, one hers) on a camping trip. Neither of them had been on an overnight trip, camping before and they were both very excited, but nervous about spending time with their new stepparent and stepsibling.*

*We had the most wonderful time—fishing in a lake, walking barefoot through a nearby mountain stream, and cooking our dinner over a fire.*

*We all bundled up in a big family sized tent and listened to the owls as we lay in our sleeping bags. It was the most amazing weekend and we really bonded as a family. The boys are already asking when the next trip will be scheduled!"*

Good luck to you and your blended family as you plan your vacations. Send us your photos and stories—we'd love to hear them!

### Question
*"How would you blend a family with kids 15, 13, 8, and 4 year old twins? They are so apart in ages—help!"*

I admit I had some help on this one. I asked my 16 & 18 year old what kinds of things they do, when they are visiting their dad, and their 3-year-old half-brother. Here's what we came up with:

- Watching kid's shows are fun. (My teenage kids can sing the songs from Bob the Builder and other TV shows, right along with their little toddler half-brother.)
- Going to a drive-in movie together, (G rated or animated.) Get out the blankets and the snacks and make it a fun evening. If the little ones fall asleep early, you can even watch a double feature (maybe PG?) after the younger ones fall asleep.
- Make your own play dough (flour, salt, oil, and food coloring) and create funny shapes together. You can find various recipes in cookbooks, the library and on the internet.
- Family night—order a pizza, rent a movie and watch it together.
- Holiday Activities—decorate the Christmas tree together, dye Easter eggs, carve pumpkins (little ones use markers or paint to decorate pumpkins)

Basically, do anything you can, together, as a family:

- Prepare the meal (little ones set the table or put out napkins)
- Clean up after dinner (little ones carry the eating utensils back to the sink)
- Wash the car
- Clean the house (little ones can "dust" and carry small loads of laundry to the laundry room)

Treat them fairly, love them all, and they will follow your example and be good siblings to each other.

## Use photography and scrapbooking to unite your blended family

Blended Families are sometimes tough to unite. One day you are two separate families, and after a brief marriage ceremony, a few bites of cake . . . the next thing you know, you're considered one family. Well—at least on the outside.

It's difficult for adults and kids to get used to the newly blended family—new stepparents, new stepsiblings, and new home—quite a lot of changes in a short time. By using photography and scrapbooking, you can creatively begin merging your family into one unit.

## Take candid photos during activities

Hauling everyone to a portrait studio is a traumatic event for a newly blended family. Sometimes kids feel it's disloyal to the other biological parent if they are photographed as a family with the new stepparent. Take informal, candid shots of your kids. Let them be silly, make faces, and enjoy the camera.

## Celebrate *any* event

Celebrate each child and adult's birthday as a family event. Recognize all holidays, even the silly ones (Ground Hog Day, Chocolate Day, Belly Laugh Day??) No, I'm not making these up, check your local library or the internet for more unusual or bizarre celebrations. Don't forget your camera!

## Put photos around the house

Choose some of the best shots and frame them. Put these photos in prominent locations around the house. You can put photos of you and your blended family in your child's room. It's also fun to create a photo wall. Put you and your new spouse in the middle, his kids on one side, and her kids on the other. You can use old photos for this—of the kids at different stages of their life, as long as these photos do not include your ex-spouse. Use the opposing wall to start putting blended photos of your group, as you catch stepsiblings together.

If you experience a little resistance, you can always purchase a frame and "put" the kids together. Example: with four kids, you would purchase a frame with four photo inserts. Put an individual photo of each child in each slot. Viola! You have all four kids together in one photo frame!

**Use scrapbooking to create a family album**
Take all of these photos and start recording your family's life. Make the album fun—with stickers, funny thoughts, and details of each event. If any child expresses interest while you are working on the album, let them write comments, next to the photos, in their own handwriting.

Label the album, "Our Family" and put the album in a well-trafficked area of your home. If kids stop and look through the album, ignore them, and let them spent some time looking at photos of their new blended family. Add to the album regularly, and continuing blending your family into a cohesive unit in this fun, creative manner.

**Create your own traditions**
You can use some traditions from your old family, but modify them a little, and they will become your new family's tradition. If an activity was really enjoyable, plan to do it again and make it a tradition. Now is the time to try some new things (volunteering at a soup kitchen over the holidays, or taking a day hike on the first day of spring.) Your blended family might want to adopt your new activity as a tradition.

We noticed that the kids were getting their fill of turkey, as they rounded the different parent's and grandparent's houses. We prepared a nontraditional Christmas dinner of grilled seafood. The kids were surprised at first, but we had a wonderful meal and have decided that seafood for Christmas will be one of our new holiday traditions.

When a child shares his memory of old family traditions, encourage the other children to share their memories. Ask how we can combine traditions to make a new one for our blended family. Then wait for their response. You may need to provide a few suggestions, but they will get the idea that things have changed, and that's not going to be so bad, once they get used to the changes.

**Bonus Ideas**

- Make homemade pizzas
- Make ice cream sundaes with all the toppings
- Cleaning out the garage or the attic together
- Go for a walk

- Rent a movie and pop popcorn
- Wash the cars
- Paint a room together
- Play board games or set up a puzzle to do
- Go to a local fair
- Do a craft together (Many ideas are on the internet and also at your local crafts stores.)

Just for fun, here's a list of—

## The top ten worst things you can do in your newly blended family

### 1—Be very affectionate with your new spouse in front of the kids

Your kids have a lot to get used to—a new stepparent, stepsiblings and a new house. But . . . having to watch dad smooching on the back of new stepmom's neck is just a little too much for your kids! Its O.K. to hold hands occasionally, but keep it all very G rated and leave the "hot and heavy" to your moments alone.

### 2—Pretend that nothing has changed

A blended family is very different from a biological family. It takes time for everyone, including the adults, to get used to this new arrangement. Assure children that they are loved and their relationship to both mom and dad has not changed—they have just added new family members.

If you pretend everything is fine and nothing has changed, your kids will change their heads in disbelief and then rear up in a dramatic rebellion of this new "pretend" family. Your family is different now, and is missing a biological parent. That's all right, but you need to talk to your kids and tell them it's going to be O.K. and you'll be with them as they get used to the new family.

### 3—Give biological children special treatment and treat step kids as second-class citizens

It's crucial that you treat all children, whether biological or step, the same. The kids are watching you carefully to see if anyone gets special treatment. Examples: house rules should apply to everyone, house rules should be in effect at all times, all birthdays should receive similar treatment, same amount of money spent, etc.

### 4—Treat your new step kids as competitors

There should not be any competitions in a blended family. Children sometimes feel that the new stepparent is a new enemy—a competitor for them. The new stepparent may feel the same way about the kids—which the step kids take time away from their new spouse. Tell everyone that there are no competitions and no threats.

### 5—Make kids the center of the family and the center of the marriage

Sometimes the reason our previous marriage failed is because kids were in the center of the relationship. Remember this mistake and keep you and your spouse in the center of this new family.

### 6—Don't give any individual time to your spouse—only have family time

As stated above, focusing only on the kids and always having family time will ruin your new marriage. Set aside time, each day to be alone with your spouse. Schedule date nights 2-4 times a month, when the children are not invited, and focus on your marriage. Children thrive in a stable and strong marriage.

### 7—Erase discipline and structure from your new blended family

Some parents believe that the kids have been through so much—divorced parents, remarriage, new homes, etc. that it's time to back down on the discipline. Children appreciate structure. Now is not the time to take the structure away, during all of these changes. Be consistent, keep house rules, develop new rules for your new family, and treat all children, biological and step children—the same. Let the biological parent take the lead in discipline, but let kids see you as a "united front."

**8—Say negative things about your ex, in front of the kids**

Keep adult matters, such as custody issues, child support and visitation arguments, away from the kids. Don't let the kids hear you complain about your ex. Your ex-spouse is their biological parent, their mom or dad. Keep kids separated from these issues.

**9—Reminisce about the past**

Don't reminisce about the past. Focus on developing new traditions with your new family, not talking about the "old days" when biological mom and dad were together.

**10—Don't give visiting kids any personal space in your new house**

Each biological and stepchild does not need his or her own bedroom, but everyone needs some personal space. Make sure even a visiting child has a place to leave their stuff, and put some personal items around.

If you avoid these *Top Ten Worst Mistakes*, you and your family are well on their way to creating a newly blended family that will grow together in time. As you read through these tips, you will see that some of the information has been mentioned in previous chapters. It is best to not skim over these important details, but to back up, reread the sections that are still giving you trouble. Give your marriage and your family the attention they deserve.

***Question***
*"My kids keep telling me they miss the "old days" and want things to be the way they were. What do I say to them?"*

Tell them that you have good memories too, but that you don't miss all of the old days; because you also have some bad memories and made a decision to change your life. These changes mean that we have a new family now, with new traditions and activities.

***Question***
*"My daughter asked me why I love my new wife, and I don't love her anymore? This is so crazy; I don't know what to say."*

Explain to your daughter that your new wife has nothing to do with your love for her. Remind her that you love her dearly, and nothing will change this. Remind her that this is not a competition; she is not competing with the new wife. She will always be your daughter and she will not be replaced due to a new wife or additional kids.

**Group Discussion**
What activities have you planned with your blended family that was very memorable for all?

What vacations have you taken with your blended family?

When you read the *Top Ten Worst Mistakes*—which of those mistakes sounded a little too familiar to you and your spouse? (Have you made a couple of these mistakes?)

What traditions have you developed with your blended family?

List some of the traditions other couple's in the group have mentioned that you would like to try:

*

*

*

*

*

## Chapter Six Notes

# Chapter Seven

## How to treat stepsiblings and new stepparent

As adults, we often forget that our children do not automatically understand how to interact with their new stepsiblings and new stepparent. When you remarried, you chose someone who you enjoy spending time with and love. Your children did not choose this person. It's important to understand the difference. Hopefully you also chose a person that is committed to loving your children and participating in their parenting.

Your children may also still be wondering if there's a chance their parents will get back together. Many children harbor these secret feelings for years. Some children hated the constant arguments of their parents and are relieved they no longer live together; but still don't understand why their parent remarried.

Here are some talking points for you to discuss this difficult topic with your kids.

### You (the kids) are not responsible for the divorce:
Mom and dad's divorce had nothing to do with you. There is nothing you can do to change the divorce. It was the adult's decision. You did nothing to cause it—nothing. It's not your fault.

Mom and dad love you the same and this will never change. You will always be our child and we will always love you.

**Parents need adult companionship**

Children are wonderful to have, but do not replace adult companionship. You enjoy being with someone your own age, and doing things with him or her. Adults are the same. Dad doesn't want you to stay home with him, and keep him company, when you can be out with your friends. It's just not the same kind of relationship—and that's why dad (or mom) remarried.

Spending time with this new mate does not take away time from you. There is time enough for both of you. Your new stepparent is an additional person in your life to love you. You may not like this, and you may even resent your new stepparent, at first—but when my new spouse decided to marry me, they agreed to marry me and also to care and love my children (you!)

Believe it or not, it's tough for them too. They aren't used to living with you, and really don't know you. Try to tell your new stepparent about yourself, your likes and dislikes, favorite things, activities, etc.—so you can get to know each other better.

**It's O.K. to like your new stepparent**

Your new stepmom is not in competition with your biological mom. You will always have only one biological mom and dad. Stepmoms and stepdads are extra—but not in a bad way. They married your mom and dad, and this helps your mom and dad be a better parent, and a happier adult.

Your mom or dad wants you to be taken care of when you are visiting the other parent. Your stepparents will be part of this. So, it's O.K. to have fun with your new stepmom or stepdad, and even like them. It doesn't hurt your relationship with your biological mom and dad, or mean that you love them any less.

You are not in competition with your new stepmom. The love your dad has for you is different from the love he has for his new wife. He can love you both without choosing between the two.

A parent's love is different from the kind of love he has for your new stepparent. You will grow into an adult, one day, and have a family of your own. Do you want your mom moving in, and living with you for companionship? Do you want your mom to move off to college with you, and hang out with you on the weekends? No—that's silly. Adults want to be with people their own age, and most adults enjoy having a special someone in their life.

### Will I ever feel better?

That's a hard question. Divorce causes a hole in your heart. It will take a while for that hole to heal. Sometimes you may even be embarrassed to let your friends know that your parents are divorced. You're not the odd one, though; half of your friend's parents are already divorced. It's O.K. to talk about your parent's divorce. It may help to talk to your friends about your experiences. If you want to talk to a counselor, I can find you someone who understands divorces and has talked with other kids about their feelings.

It's hard to understand why mom and dad don't want to live together anymore, but it's our decision. You may never know all the details, and that's O.K. You just need to trust mom and dad to take care of you and your needs, while we continue to make the adult decisions.

### Summary

Communication is very important, especially when kids are going through so many changes. Keep the adult decisions and the adult conversations among the adults—but also remember to keep the kids informed about the new realities in their life, changes coming, and your expectations.

This is all new to your kids. Explain that you love your new spouse and understand they may not love or even like their new stepparent, immediately, and that's O.K. Remind your kids that, in your home, it is your expectation they will be polite and respectful to your new spouse. This person is an adult in your home, and is an authority over them. As mentioned before in the parenting chapter, the biological parent should take the lead in any discipline, leaving your new spouse to get to know your kids and develop a relationship with them.

Your children haven't been in this situation before. The only way they will learn how to respond to this situation is for you to guide and direct them. They won't understand it all, at first, and they will try to push a little, to see if they don't really have to follow your direction. Be firm, loving and consistent, as you continue to teach them your expectations.

## Expectations

Clearly explain to your children your expectations of their behavior:

- Treat your new step-parent with respect and politeness
- Treat your new step-siblings with politeness and kindness
- Treat everyone the way you would like to be treated
- Interact with the entire family when you are here

The last entry discussing "interacting with the entire family" means that they cannot direct all conversation exclusively to their biological parent and ignore everyone else in the house. They must speak to anyone else living or visiting your home, while they are there. Children may not be experts at starting conversations, but they can invite their stepsiblings to participate in their activities, and ask about their interests. You may have to start some of these conversations, during meals, or other casual times when you're all together, to assist your kids in getting to know each other.

Children need to understand that your new spouse does not take the place of their other parent; but is an adult and parent in this family. Your new spouse is another adult who will love them and care for them. Liking this new spouse does not mean that they love their biological parents any less.

## Create opportunities

Create opportunities for your new spouse to get to know your children. At meals, you can share information about your children and encourage your children to elaborate. You may be comfortable with the silence, but your new spouse will appreciate a little assistance in getting to know your kids. Here are some examples:

> "Joseph really enjoys soccer and soccer season is starting next week. Do you have any games coming up Joseph?"

> "Claire is getting really good at playing the piano. I'd love it if you could play a piece for us after dinner Claire."

**Personal Space**

Provide personal space for everyone in your house. Your visiting children may need to share a room, or you may need to convert a basement to a bedroom, or a section of a playroom to a sleeping area, during their visits. Just remember that personal space is very important. Your child needs to have a place they can go, shut the door, and just relax. Ideally, a room for each child is best—but not always economically feasible.

Talk with each child about having some personal space in your house. If possible, let them make personal choices in their area such as room color, comforter, curtains or accessories. Figure out how to make the room or area comfortable for your child. If possible, have this area "untouched" by the other kids, while they are gone, so that they know this is truly their space. Encourage your visiting child to leave clothes or other items in your home to make their transition back and forth between the houses easier.

When designing space for all of your children (especially those who only visit) consider:

- A closet or chest of drawers to store their things
- Some toiletries in the bathroom—such as a toothbrush, hairbrush and shampoo
- Personalized items that show this space is their space
- A clock
- Different bathrooms for the different (non-related) sexes

**Bonus Idea**

Put up a photo collage of your child in his room. This collage should include candid, informal photos of your family, in this home, having fun times. If a child lives with you full time, they should be allowed to put photos of the other biological parent in their room. (A visiting child can keep photos of the other biological parent in their full time home.)

**Question**

*"We are selling our houses and purchasing a new house. What should we consider with our newly blended family?"*

Space for everyone is essential—separate rooms are best, but not always possible. Involve your children in the process. Ask your kids what they consider important in a new home. Take the children with you on some of your house hunting adventures.

Involve the children in your house hunting. This shows them that you value their input and their opinion. Stress that this new home will also be their home. Remember, though—ultimately you and your spouse must make the decision of which home best for you.

### Question
*"Help! All of our kids (both his and mine) are ganging up on us about one of our new house rules. What should we do?"*

Congratulations! Your kids are well on their way to becoming a family. Uniting against the parents is a truly bonding event! Sorry for the humor, but it is truly a moment to celebrate. But, bonding aside, I wouldn't worry much. Children naturally will test boundaries and rules to see if you are serious. Make sure you are a united front with the kids, and be prepared to enforce consequences if they disobey your new house rule.

### Group Discussion
Share activities you've used to get your step kids and biological kids to interact with each other.

*

*

*

*

*

Share some experiences about how you get your kids to talk to the rest of the blended family during their visits to your home

Discuss ways you help your spouse get to know your kids.

*

*

*

*

*

*

Share some experiences about how you get your kids to talk to the rest of the blended family during their visits to your home

Tell the group ways you have personalized kid's rooms and/or provided space for each of your children.

Discuss how you have worked through the "bathroom issues"—of separating the boys and the girls in your blended family.

# Chapter Seven Notes

_____

_____

_____

_____

_____

_____

_____

_____

_____

_____

_____

_____

_____

_____

_____

_____

_____

_____

_____

_____

_____

_____

_____

# Chapter Eight

## Visits to your house and the other parent's house

It's your job as adults, to assist your kids with visits from your house to the other parent's house. Be positive and help them transition between the two houses.

Do you have trouble when your child returns from your ex's house? The little ones may call dad "mom" for the first day or so (or the other way around.) That's fine, and just answer them without acting as if you noticed.

The more difficult struggles with your child may be with the differences in house rules and life styles. It may be helpful to remind them, a day before or on the drive to your house, about your expectations for them when they are in your home. Remind them how mom and dad's houses may be different, but you need to remember our expectations when you are visiting us.

Remember to keep your house rules consistent with every child, whether living there full time or visiting. Also, once you have established these house rules, don't modify or change them (unless you see a real need) because this will cause confusion in your children as they learn your expectations.

### No negative talk
Do not speak negatively about your ex-spouse in front of your child. This person is your child's other biological parent. Speaking negatively does not help your child adapt to the new situation and also creates confusing feelings,

as the child tries to decide if he is supposed to take sides in the battles between his parents.

### Planning successful visitation for your child

You and your ex should have a written agreement about visitation. This should be fair to all and also have some flexibility to it.

Are you ready for the summer, the new school year, and the holidays? At least 3-4 times a year, you and your ex need to reconfirm your schedules and your children's visitation. Keep a large calendar with all the visitation dates marked.

It can become very complicated if *you* have remarried, and your new *spouse's ex* has remarried, and *your* ex-spouse has remarried . . . Did you follow all that? You will be communicating with a possible total of five families or more!

### Tips for successful visitation schedules:

- Plan ahead
- Clearly communicate your expectations
- Be flexible and willing to change a couple of weekends to accommodate the majority—or a special event in another family
- Don't take these changes personally. Sometimes we believe changes in the visitation schedule are attempts of our ex-spouse to ruin our plans. Even if this is true (and I sincerely hope it is not) then just "take the high road," assume that their changes are necessary, and be flexible.

### Expressing expectations to your child when they return to your home:

- Be positive
- Be consistent (keep the rules the same)
- Remind them of what they need to improve, but tell them how proud you are of them for the recent improvements they have already made
- Be positive!

### Question
*"My child is afraid to talk about visits to their other biological parent's house. My child is afraid I'll be jealous. What should I do?"*

It's natural for your child to not know the "rules" and expectations in the new arrangement. They may be afraid that you will be upset when they talk about how much fun they had last weekend with your ex.

Help your child understand that you love them and want the best for them. Time with the other parent is wonderful, and you would love to hear about their time with the other parent.

Some children will be suspicious of this, at first, especially if you had a messy divorce. Keep your inquiries simple: "How was the weekend with dad? Did you have fun?" Then wait . . . if your child wants to tell you more; let them. Don't judge, frown or ask detailed questions (or the sharing will stop.) This isn't time to spy on your ex; it's time to let your child know you are interested in him and his experiences.

## Never use the child as a messenger
Never send messages through your child. In today's world of technology, we have phones, email and text messages. There is no reason for you to send a message through your child. By communicating through your child, you literally put your child in the middle. Separate children from adult conflict, and reassure them that your love for them has not changed. Even though mommy and daddy live in different places now, they both love you.

## Be Positive!
Yes—I know I am repeating myself, but I can't emphasize enough the importance of being positive, and not speaking negatively of your ex. Even if your child arrives with juicy stories of terrible things your ex has said about you; respond to your child positively, with statements such as, "I don't want to hear anymore. I won't speak negatively about your mom and I would hope that she will not speak negatively about me." I know this is hard, but set a good example for your children. It also may shame your ex into watching their words too!

**Time to talk**
When you are in the car, or involved in another activity, ask your child how things are going. Just pause and wait. Let them know that you realize all the changes are difficult, but you are always willing to listen. Then—do just that . . . listen.

**Disney dad syndrome**
Your child will be traveling back and forth between houses. This isn't the time to try to out-do your ex with elaborate activities. Visits with your children should be normal family time. If you have errands to run on Saturday, take your visiting child with you. You may want to stop for some ice cream, but your whole day should not revolve around the visiting child. Planning a little undivided attention over the visiting weekend is fine, as long as it doesn't separate you, for hours at a time, from your spouse and the other children. These types of visits aren't normal, and the child should not expect to have a personalized vacation with their non-custodial parent at every visit.

The other extreme would be to ignore the visit. Try not to schedule long events that would keep your (older) child at home alone or with a baby sitter (for the younger child) while you attend an activity during their visiting weekend. Find a balance between special weekend events, and enjoying yourself as a couple and as a blended family. Planning simple events with your entire family are the best way to blend your family.

You will find that children enjoy the simple things as much as the expensive events as long as we are giving them our attention, listening to their stories and sharing our lives with them.

**Bonus idea**
Purchase each child in your family a small weekly planner so that they can watch the calendar and understand which weekends they will be spending with you. All ages of children are confused about the switching back and forth between houses. This gives the younger child a sense of continuity and the older child the opportunity to plan their own schedule of activities around the visits to mom and dad.

Remind your child that the weekends (or time) they spend with you, they are under your house rules. Request that all activities should be discussed with the parents in this house for permission, before scheduling.

**Extra bonus idea—monthly check-in date with your child**
Arrange a time, once a month, for you to spend a few minutes alone with your child. This could be a drive for an ice cream, hot chocolate or a lunch in a low to moderately priced restaurant. Tell them that this is your time to check in. You can make this a different time than their regular visitation (if possible) and just pick them up for an hour.

**Couple Time**
Think of times when you both had to rise above the negativity of your ex-spouse and ignore the gossip you hear from the kids.

Discuss how you can support your spouse when they are experiencing negative talk from their ex.

Talk with your spouse about how to plan a balance between one-on-one time when the visiting child is here, couple's time and family time. Make sure you both compromise and negotiate until both feel the balance is fair.

**Group Time**
Discuss how you rise above the gossip and negative talk of your ex-spouse.

What are tips you can give the group about how you assist your child(ren) in transitioning between the houses?

Discuss how you create a balance between family time, one-on-one time with your visiting child, and couple time:

## Chapter Eight Notes

# Section Three

# Your Ex-Spouse, Parents and the Rest of the World

# Chapter Nine

## Maintaining a positive relationship with your ex-spouse

You have divorced your ex, but he or she will remain a part of your life because of the children. Remember, it takes both parents to raise your children. This requires you to continue a reasonable amount of communication with your spouse. The relationship has changed though, and you need to set new boundaries.

### Keep contact to a minimum

Do not contact your ex-spouse unless you have a topic related to the children. One phone call a day is excessive, several text messages a day is extremely excessive. Speak briefly and clearly when you have a question or issue about the children. Emails are better than phone calls, if your issue is not an emergency. Emails allow you to reread your message before sending. You also have a written copy of all communication if there are still legal battles between you and your ex-spouse.

You no longer have a relationship with this person, except that he or she is the other parent of your children. Your only relationship is one of co-parenting. Asking for assistance with household repairs, meals, or even just talking about your day—is no longer acceptable.

Some blended families are able to become friends with their ex-spouses and their new mates. I've been told of couples who have cookouts together and celebrate the holidays together as one, big extended family. This situation is quite unusual, though, and in the beginning of your new marriage, it's not time to try to establish these friendships. Concentrate on your marriage, and leave the conversation with your ex-spouse dedicated to discussions about the children.

**Do not speak negatively about your ex-spouse in front of the children.**
Yes—I've said this before, but some may not understand its importance!

It doesn't make you look better in front of the kids, and it does not help with the co-parenting relationship you have with your ex. Children are confused by negative talk and should not be trapped in the middle of your marital issues.

**Don't send messages to your ex-spouse through the kids**
Your children have been through some major changes—mom and dad not living together, the divorce, and now visitation back and forth between the houses. They do not need to be involved in adult discussions or arguments.

**Don't question the kids about their activities when they return from a visit with the other parent.**
Children are very suspicious of this and wonder what they are supposed to say. They wonder if it's O.K. to have fun at dad's house. You want your children to have a positive relationship with their daddy, and want them to feel that they don't have to report back all the activity going on in his house. It's O.K. to ask them if they had a good time over the weekend, and then smile and say, "great" after their brief response. Move on to another topic, immediately after the question, so that the kids know its O.K. to have enjoyed the time, and that you're not being nosy about their dad.

**Work together with your ex to coordinate a visitation schedule for the kids.**
Let your ex know if there are any changes to your schedule, as soon as possible. Emergencies will arise (for both parties) but planning ahead allows both parents to care for the kids as best as possible.

**Don't sabotage family events at your ex's house.**
You may be considering planning a huge meal to serve to your kid's right before dropping them off for Thanksgiving dinner at your ex's house; or bringing them to their other parent's house, late, so that they miss an important event scheduled for them by your ex-spouse. You may think these tactics hurt your

ex, but in reality, you are only hurting your own children. Step back, and remember to do what's best for your kids.

**Don't speak negatively about your ex's new partner.**
This is the person who will help raise your children. This person is caring for your children when they are not with you.

Speak positively to your ex and make sure they know that you are not saying any negative things about them to the children. Communicate with your ex that you also expect them to remain positive when speaking to the children. If your ex remarries, do not speak negatively about the new stepparent. This is an excellent time for you to show cooperation with your ex, by helping your children adjust to the new stepparent.

I know it's difficult to remain silent about your ex-spouse's new mate. It's natural to make comparisons, and even feel a little jealous, even if you are no longer interested in your ex-spouse. But, hold your tongue! Your child needs to develop a positive relationship with this new stepparent. Speaking negatively or calling the new stepparent by a nickname does not help your child adjust to the new blended family.

I can't stress enough that speaking negatively about your ex, or her new spouse, in front of your children is not a good practice. These negative words upset, confuse and hurt your children. You have your spouse to vent to, if you really need to talk. This is another reason to make couple's time a priority in your marriage. Keep your children out of the conflicts.

**Visitation**
Decide on a reasonable visitation schedule. This should have been taken care of during your separation, but if not, discuss this immediately. The children need a schedule to depend upon and organize their life around. Once the schedule is in place, do your best to keep it. If your ex requests a change, listen to their reasoning and try to be flexible, if possible. Your cooperation with your ex may confuse them, at first, but when they realize that your goal is to do what's best for your child, they can either join you, or argue with themselves in futility.

If you have a change, let them know about it as soon as possible. Give your ex a brief description of the event and the need for you to change the visitation.

You don't need to provide all the personal details, but enough for your ex to understand that a schedule change is really necessary.

### Keep your ex informed

If you know about school or other events your child is involved in make sure you communicate these events to your ex (the non-custodial parent.) Send copies of school report cards, access to any websites, and announcements of meetings that involve your child to your ex. Keep your ex involved in your child's life. This supports your child and is the right thing to do.

This is not a control issue. Keeping information about your child away from the other parent only hurts your child. Work cooperatively with your ex-spouse to provide any relevant information about your child in a timely manner.

### Choose your battles

If possible, be flexible if your ex asks to make a change in the schedule. Once or twice is fine, and is not worth getting upset about. Save your energy for issues that really matter; issues about parenting your children or making major decisions about them. Talk with your new spouse about these issues. Your new spouse can help you decide if a particular issue is worth really arguing with your ex about, or if this is one of the ones you let go. Always keep your new spouse informed about discussions with your ex. Remember, you and your new spouse are the core, the center of the relationship. You should not have any secrets from your new spouse.

There shouldn't be any reason to talk with your ex privately. If your ex does call you on the phone, talk to your ex in front of your spouse. (If the children are present, and you think the conversation may be unpleasant, go into another room.) Your spouse should not feel left out of any conversations with your ex. Yes—the biological parents should make the decisions related to their child, but now you are married and your new spouse should have a part in any decisions affecting *your life*. Some families are able to create very close co-parenting experiences in which all parents (biological and step) communicate regularly. While I don't recommend this for every family, don't see your ex and her spouse as the enemy—but as partners in raising your children. Co-parenting requires some extra effort, but is crucial to the emotional health of your kids.

**Keep it sane**
Don't take your ex-spouse's emotions personally. Sometimes your ex will express inappropriate or exaggerated feelings. An example may be that you can't show up for your son's softball game, and this results in a ten-minute yelling, screaming message left on your answering machine. Just step away from the emotions, and realize she is expressing her feelings that you are not attending the event, and believes your son will be disappointed. These feelings are O.K.—but not the yelling and screaming. Don't respond to these exaggerated emotions—just let it go.

**Keep it focused on the kids**
Communication should be limited to conversations about the kids. It's no longer necessary to share day-to-day events with your ex, vent about your day, or talk about anything not related to your kids. Your relationship with you ex is now based solely on the kids.

**Keep it organized**
Prepare a visitation calendar in advance. Follow the guidelines set by your separation agreement and schedule special events as far in advance as possible. Kids like to know where they are going to be. It's helpful to give each child a pocket calendar so they can keep up with their visits to mom and dad.

**Keep it fair**
Remember you are doing what's best for the kids by arranging time with both mom and dad. Don't cheat your ex out of visitation, nor should you opt-out of your assigned time.

Holidays: remember to alternate the holidays each year. Reassure your kids that Christmas on the 26th, or their birthday on the following Saturday, is still a special event. Make it fun to switch the days, and still enjoy the holidays together.

I don't encourage families to celebrate Christmas or birthdays with their ex-spouse because it confuses the children, especially if one or both of the parents has not remarried. The children see everyone being friendly and civil and wonder why mom and dad can't get married again.

Gifts: communicate with your ex that you want to treat all children fairly. Discuss your expectations for birthdays and other holiday gifts. You can't control what your ex-spouse does, but at least you can positively and calmly communicate your expectations and reasoning.

Stress with your ex and your child(ren) that, in this house, all children (stepchildren or biological children) will be treated fairly and equally—they can depend on it. You will be surprised how much your child will relax when she realizes that there is no competition on love, attention, rewards or gifts in your house.

### Keep it flexible

Things happen, and unexpected events may arrive at the last minute. Be flexible if your ex wants to change the visitation schedule. If you notice this happens frequently, remind him you need at least a month's notice to properly rearrange your schedule. With a month's notice, convey that you will be happy to make the changes. When emergencies or special events pop up, both mom and dad will need to flex their schedules to accommodate.

Do not make any changes to your family's schedule without consulting your spouse. You can talk, or exchange emails with your ex-spouse, but don't commit to any changes in the schedule until you have discussed these changes with your spouse. Your spouse should be your focus, the center of the marriage and the center of your family. Your spouse is your teammate in all of this, and the one who is on your side, helping you make decisions to do what is best for all of your family. Keep your spouse informed about possible upcoming changes.

Remember to do what's best for your kids. Talk with them, ask them about their upcoming events and encourage them to keep you informed so that you can stay an active part of their lives.

### Question
*"My ex keeps calling me, she wants me to fix things, and also listen to her talk when she's had a bad day—what can I do to stop this?"*

If she calls, let it go to voicemail. If the message does not relate to the children—return all voicemails, emails and text messages with the same consistent message, "We are no longer married and I'm not in your life except when it relates to our children. Please do not contact me unless it's to discuss our children. I wish you well, but I have moved on."

### Question
*"My ex leaves me long, screaming messages about the kids. What should I do?"*

Try not to take it personally. Settle down and listen or read the message calmly. You can reply, but make sure you are not responding by attacking back.

Stick with the facts—the needs and schedules of the kids. Try to be reasonable and calm, and do not respond to the emotions of the message.

### Couple's Time
Discuss with your spouse conversations you have had this week with your ex-spouse.

If you believe your mate spends too much time in conversations with her ex, talk with her and figure out if there is a need for such extensive talks.

What arrangements have you and your spouse made for the coming holidays (birthday, etc.)?

**Group Discussion**

How do you communicate to your ex-spouse that there is too much non-children related talk?

Do you and your mate talk with your ex-spouse together on the telephone?

What subjects are discussed during the conversations with the ex? How can these subjects be shortened?

# Chapter Nine Notes

# Chapter Ten

## Managing our expectations and the expectations of those in our family

I regularly hear from stepmoms and stepdads:

> *"My step kids never remember my birthday, Father's Day or Mother's Day, and don't even buy me a gift for Christmas!"*

Unfortunately—I place the source of this problem onto the biological parent in the house. How else will kids know to honor their new stepparent if the biological parent doesn't guide them?

**Tip:** If the kids in the home are under 18, or still in college, then the stepparent is helping to co-parent the kids. If the stepparent is co-parenting, then they should be honored on Mother's Day or Father's Day. Honoring their stepmother or stepfather does not take away from their biological mother or father. Each stepparent works very hard, all year to help you co-parent their child, sometimes without any recognition or thanks from your child.

All stepparents should be honored on their birthday because they married into the family and are now an adult in this home, a part of the family, and someone to be remembered at birthdays and other holidays. Would you ever forget a child's birthday? Never forget your spouse! Remind your children, both biological and step, that their stepparent's birthday is coming soon, and make plans to celebrate the event as a family.

**Question**
*"My kids adamantly refuse to honor my new wife for Mother's Day and her birthday, what should I do?"*

As you read above, it's the biological dad's responsibility to teach your kids to honor your wife for Mother's Day and her birthday. Tell the kids that honoring their stepmom does not compete in any way with their mother. Remind them of the things your wife does for them, all year. Also, tell them that their own birthday gift comes from you and their new stepmom, and she is part of our family now and one to be remembered on special days. Remember, the parents are in charge, not the kids. It's your responsibility as a parent to train your children and teach them your expectations about honoring the adults in your home.

**Question**
*"What about Christmas? Do my kids need to buy their new stepdad a gift?"*

Again, the biological parent should be guiding the children. When organizing the gift giving, make sure everyone is remembered in your blended family, with even little ones giving gifts to their siblings. Cost of gifts doesn't matter; it's that everyone is exchanging gifts as a family. Little ones can make crafts or draw pictures, older ones can create coupon books for gifts. It truly is the parent's responsibility to guide your children. You have guided your kids for years, and now they are in a blended family, which is unfamiliar territory to them. Talk with them about your expectations and help them honor your spouse and their stepparent.

**Question**
*"My kids say that my new spouse is 'Mom's new husband, but he's not my stepdad,' how do I get them to acknowledge their stepdad on his birthday and Father's Day?"*

I understand older kids (over age 21) saying that they don't need a parent. If they are living on their own, and you truly aren't participating in the parenting process (although I believe we parent our children far into their 20's!) then talk with your adult child about this. If they aren't being parented, then they still need to honor your new spouse on birthdays and holidays, because he is a member of your family. Remind them that your new spouse married into this family, and you will accept their spouse, when they marry, even though their new spouse won't be related to the family. Teach your adult children about blended families and inclusiveness. It's important to start now, before the grandchildren are born and the little ones are told that some of your grandparents are "real" and some are "not real grandparents." Stop this behavior, right now, and teach your kids about how to be inclusive in their blended family. Remember what's best for your children and keep these conflicts away from them. An extra parent or grandparent provides more love for your child—this is not an opportunity to exclude a grandparent from your child's life.

## Grandparents

*The Grandparents Golden Rules to Blended Family* is included as a bonus at the end of this book. Remember that ultimately it is the responsibility of the biological parent to inform his or her parents or adult siblings of the new spouse's birthday, and remind them to include their new spouse in any holiday gift giving.

I was amazed and very appreciative when my new mother-in-law very warmly welcomed my kids and me into her family at Christmas. My husband and I married on December 1st, and had a rush of purchasing and moving into a new house, decorating (on the afternoon of the wedding,) me and my kids moving in the next day, and then jumping head first into the holidays as a newly blended family. (And yes—if you were wondering, our furniture wasn't all in the right house, but we did manage to spend our wedding night, together, without kids, and had a delayed honeymoon several months later!)

Much to my surprise, a couple of weeks later, and a package arrived. Inside were homemade goodies addressed to my kids, and a card and metal container addressed to my kids and me. Inside were nametags, inviting us to the next family reunion!

My new mother-in-law had put together a welcome package with baked goodies, a copy of the family tree (with my name and my kid's names added!) and a short note explaining that her family has a reunion every year. She included nametags for us to attend the next event! All of this love and consideration for my kids and me brought squeals of joy from my kids (the baked goods) and tears to my eyes (from the other precious items in the box.)

On a side note: imagine my surprise when I discovered that her yearly "Carter Family Reunion" (her maiden name) was also my maternal grandmother's maiden name. My grandmother's family in North Carolina has a similar reunion to the one my mother-in-law has in Tennessee. My husband and I found out that we could possibly be distant cousins! Another bonding moment occurred as we shared this fact with our kids and received a collective "gross" from all of our teenagers—biological and step alike!

My new mother-in-law also prepared envelopes (equal size, shape and decoration) for my husband and me, and all five kids, with their names on it, to be put under the tree as Christmas gifts. Yes—all the kid's gift amounts were the same (my husband and I looked at the checks.) In conclusion, some grandparents will naturally know how to blend with your new family, and some will need more instruction. It's the same with parents—we just need a little help figuring out how to blend our family and do what's best.

### Couple Time
Discuss how you are going to talk with your extended family about how to include your new spouse and step kids into the holiday events.

**Group Discussion**

What steps have you taken to introduce your blended family to your relatives?

How do you remind relatives of an upcoming birthday for your spouse or step child?

## Chapter Ten Notes

# Conclusion

## For a successful blended family, keep your spouse in the center of your marriage

Devote the majority of your blended family time to creating and maintaining a healthy marriage. Your kids will thrive in this stable and loving environment.

### Question
*"If I focus on my marriage and my spouse, how will I know that she wants what's best for my kids? Am I neglecting my kids if I focus on her?"*

If you married someone who would be a good spouse and a good parent to your kids, and they love you, then I would not worry. The two of you will do what's best for your family and that includes your biological kids. Don't think of your family as "us" and "them." Your wife and you are in the center, and from the center—the core—of the family, you will make the best decisions for all of your family—biological and step.

### Question
*"I'm afraid I can't make my kids happy if I always put my wife first. My kids think I love my wife more than I love them."*

Remind your kids that this is not a competition—they are not in competition with your new spouse. Your love for your mate is different from your parental love for your children. Loving your mate and putting your mate in the center of the marriage and the family does

119

not hurt your kids. Help your kids see you and your new spouse as a unit. When you make decisions with your spouse, present them to your kids together. Tell your kids that you and your spouse will work together to do what's best for them. Let your kids see their parent and stepparent as a team, working *for* them, and doing what's best for them, as a parenting couple.

### Create your own memories
Schedule trips to take—just you and your spouse. These trips may be elaborate vacations, or just a drive to the local flea market. If you enjoy an activity; find time to do it again.

It's O.K. to talk about the past and share some activities you would like to experience again. You can share these pleasant events without talking about your ex. It's also O.K. to talk about activities you've always wanted to try, but never have taken the time. If your spouse is interested, figure out how to try out this new activity. You may surprise yourself with a new youthful spirit, as you venture into the world with new eyes and a new attitude for life!

Get to know your spouse. Don't assume that she likes all the same things your ex likes—ask her! Share your favorite foods, restaurants and activities—then ask her to share her favorites. Don't assume he wants to do the same house chores your ex did. Talk about it and figure it out together!

### Be thankful
Remember to thank your spouse on a regular basis. Make sure your mate understands how much you appreciate them. It's the little things that are sometimes ignored: fixing breakfast for the family, doing the laundry, taking out the trash, mowing the lawn, and arranging a weekend movie.

### Your new spouse can't read your mind!
You may have been in a marriage for years, or maybe you have lived on your own for a while. Either way—your new spouse cannot read your mind! If you have a misunderstanding, stop and think about whether you fully communicated your intentions. Sometimes a little extra communication will prevent conflicts. Ask your spouse's opinion and preferences, regularly. You have a new relationship, and this relationship will take work. Remember to keep this marriage a priority, give it time, energy, and it will be a strong, lasting marriage.

**Bonus activities to do together, just the two of you:**

- Ride bikes
- Take a walk
- Go shopping (the mall, yard sales, flea markets, seasonal events)
- Start a house improvement project together
- Take a bath together
- Read the same book and then share your thoughts about the book
- Enroll in a class together

**Keys to a successful blended family:**

- Focus on your spouse (Remember the diagrams?)
- Keep your marriage in the center of the family
- Develop house rules and expectations for all of your children
- Co-parent, and the biological parent leads in the discipline
- Communicate, guide and teach expectations to your kids, ex-spouses and others
- Don't get defensive when emotions arise
- Remember, even biological families have bad days—so your family isn't perfect either
- Look for humor in life and your blending

**Ask yourself these questions regularly to make sure you are staying on track in your blended family:**

Am I keeping my spouse in the center of my marriage and my family?

Am I keeping my spouse informed about decisions related to the kids?

Do I try, every day, to look at our family as a unit, and not "my kids" and "his kids?"

Do I treat my ex-spouse with respect and kindness?

Do I rise above the negative talk and behavior when I interact with my ex-spouse?

Do I try to not be defensive when my ex-spouse is angry, and keep the conversation directly related to our kids?

Do I keep my children out of the adult conflicts?

Have I consistently treated all my kids, both biological and step, equally and fairly?

Do I allow my spouse to take the lead, when disciplining her biological children?

Do I provide equal consequences when my kids, both biological and step, do not obey our house rules?

**Couple's Time**
Talk with your spouse about some of your favorite activities. Then ask your spouse to share his/her favorites. Figure out some interests or hobbies you can do together.

What is a healthy activity you and you spouse can do together?

**Group Discussion**
Share with the group some of the activities you have done with your spouse, and some future activities you want to try together.

Give some examples of this week when you and your spouse worked together to solve a blended family issue.

What are some healthy activities you and your spouse do together or will commit to try together? Share with the group your start date.

**Special note from Shirley Cress Dudley:**
Some blended families may need extra assistance in addition to this book. If so, please seek counseling in your local area to assist you. Look for someone who specializes in blended families, or at least, specializes in marriage and family counseling. I also offer telephone coaching for blended couples who prefer this type of assistance. Check out the *Blended Family Advice* website for more information.

This book contains no legal advice. Consult your attorney for any legal information or decisions that concern your blended family.

Good luck blending your family! I would love to hear your experiences, struggles and joys!

**Shirley Cress Dudley**
Shirley@BlendedFamilyAdvice.com
Founder of The Blended and Step Family Resource Center
www.TheBlendedandStepFamilyResourceCenter.com

# Abbreviations and other weird things about blended families

The internet is a wonderful thing, but can be confusing at times. The more I started searching around looking for information on blended families and stepfamilies, the more information I found. I also discovered that we're not sure what to call ourselves—blended or stepfamilies. It doesn't really matter—whatever is more comfortable for your family, as long as you see yourselves as one unit.

While researching blended families, I had trouble understanding some of the information on the internet because it seemed to be written in code! At first, I couldn't figure it out, and then as I read the context, some of it started to make sense.

I noticed that stepfamilies like to vent. Surprised? Guess not! It's tough out there, and it helps to talk to others who understand your situation. Many stepmoms and stepdads use the internet to talk about their blended family issues. Just remember, the internet has public access, and your online venting about the latest crazy behavior of your stepdaughter can easily be read by your stepdaughter or her friends!

I also learned that stepparents who vent on the internet like to communicate in abbreviations! So, if you're a new stepparent, let me teach you the stepparent code, so that you too can communicate on the internet with other parents, and talk to them in their own "language."

## Step Parent's Code

> Bio= biological
>
> Step= stepparent, stepmom, stepdad, etc.

OK, now it gets harder . . .

> BM= biological mom
>
> BD= biological dad
>
> BS= biological son
>
> BD= biological daughter
>
> SM= stepmom
>
> SD= stepdad or stepdaughter (oh dear!)
>
> SS= stepson
>
> BF= boyfriend or sometimes biological father (yikes!)

And more . . .

> POA= power of attorney
>
> CS= child support
>
> MIL= mother in law
>
> FIL=father in law
>
> Skids= step-kids (A funny one, but I actually did see this one used.)

Now you can use these abbreviations and speak in "code" to other stepparents on blogs, forums and other blended and step family sites.

# Notes

## Notes

# Bonus Material

# Blended Family Financial Planner

Blended Couple Financial Pledge:

- Together, we will figure out a way to meet all of our financial needs
- Together we will provide for our blended family
- We will honestly discuss our goals and dreams
- If something isn't working, we will come together and re-discuss our plan

His Signature:

_____ Date: _____

Her Signature:

_____ Date: _____

**Top financial priorities for the *12 months*:**

| His: | Hers: |
|------|-------|
| 1 | 1 |
| 2 | 2 |
| 3 | 3 |
| 4 | 4 |
| 5 | 5 |

**Top financial priorities for the *next 5 years*:**

| His: | Hers: |
|------|-------|
| 1 | 1 |
| 2 | 2 |
| 3 | 3 |
| 4 | 4 |
| 5 | 5 |

**Top financial priorities for the *next 10 years*:**

| His: | Hers: |
|------|-------|
| 1 | 1 |
| 2 | 2 |
| 3 | 3 |
| 4 | 4 |
| 5 | 5 |

## $$$ Discussion

Compare the similarities and differences in your goals. Decide upon your top 3 priorities as a couple.

**Our Top financial priorities for the *12 months*:**
1
2
3

**Our Top financial priorities for the *next 5 years*:**
1
2
3

**Our Top financial priorities for the *next 10 years*:**
1
2
3

**Notes:**

### *$$$ Discussion*

How much debt did you each bring into the marriage?

His Debt _____

Her Debt _____

What are your goals for paying off these debts?

His Goals _____

Her Goals _____

**Notes:**

## $$$ Discussion

What amount of money is "free" to spend on a weekly basis?

_$_____

Examples of what this money is used for:

-
-
-
-
-

*Any amount over this sum needs to be discussed.

**Notes:**

# Budget

Create a spreadsheet that will assist you in planning your family budget. There are many examples on the internet; several of which are free.

*You will want to include:*

- Your incomes
- Child Support (as income or as an expense)
- Utilities (gas, water, electricity, cable, internet, telephone and cell phones)
- Mortgage or Rent (insurance)
- Groceries and household supplies
- Auto insurance
- Car payment(s)
- Auto expenses: gas, repairs/maintenance
- Insurance: Health, dental, vision, life
- Education: tuition, childcare expenses
- Entertainment: movies, plays, dining out, travel
- Children's allowance and other expenses
- Savings each month: savings account, retirement account)
- Donations
- Miscellaneous (anything else you can think of that is a monthly expense)

### $$$ Additional Discussions
**Take your time and discuss issues and expectations about the various subjects:**

- Private vs. public schools and who pays for them?

- College expenses for each child?

- Clothes (kids grow!) and shoes

# Successful Blended Family Holidays

Yikes—the holidays are coming and I have a newly blended family!

Many parents would be nervous about the holidays approaching and how to share these events with their newly blended families. Your children and stepchildren are nervous and do not know what to expect. You are unfamiliar with their experiences and you, too, imagine the upcoming holiday season to be a time of uncertainty.

Actually, the holidays are a wonderful time to begin truly blending your family. It is a great time to develop new traditions, recognize all family members and create memories to last a lifetime.

So, begin this special report with a spirit of optimism, knowing that the holiday season is going to build bonds in your blended family, create memories, and traditions, and give your children and stepchildren guidance in how to treat this newly blended family of yours. This report is compiled of many of the questions I receive from newly blended families, asking about how to successfully celebrate the holidays. I hope the answers will help your family develop their own traditions and look forward to the holidays.

I wish you and your family a very enjoyable holiday season!

## Prepare emotionally for the holidays
The holidays can be a time of great stress and also depression for both adults and children. Memories of the past, both positive and negative, can bring sadness into your newly blended family.

## Talk about the pain
Children sometimes have trouble expressing their emotions. Little ones may "act out" instead of being able to express their feelings. For younger children, it's helpful for parents to talk to them and explain that—"I know things are different this year, and everything's a bit unfamiliar. Your mom and I still love you very much. The holidays will be different, and we aren't married anymore, but you are still loved."

Older kids and teenagers may be able to discuss their feelings. They may ask if mom and dad can celebrate the holidays together. If either of their parents has not remarried, this is very confusing for the kids, and gives the impression that mom and dad could reunite one day. Don't celebrate together unless both parents have remarried and you are able to have a happy, civil holiday together.

## Be prepared for your ex-spouse to have extra holiday emotions
Your ex-spouse may also be sensitive around the holidays. Small events, such as changing the visitation schedule by a couple of hours may set your ex-spouse into a tizzy. Take a deep breath, and don't get defensive. Remember that everyone has heightened emotions around the holidays. Try to communicate by text or email, instead of picking up the phone to hear an ex-spouse yelling on the line.

## Don't stress about the details
Everything will not work out perfectly. The kids may transition to your home late, the turkey may not cook completely, or your ex-spouse may even sabotage your holiday meal by stuffing the kids with sweets right before dropping them off to your house. It's O.K.—really! Just try to relax, life isn't normally perfect, so don't expect your holidays to be completely perfect either.

## It just gets easier
As the years pass, it will become easier and easier for your blended family to celebrate the holidays together. Children will learn what's expected of them, memorize the rotation (Am I at mom or dad's house the week before

Christmas?) and become accustomed to celebrating with their stepsiblings and stepparents.

## Do we have to celebrate on the exact day?

### Question:
*"My ex-spouse gets my kids every other holiday. This holiday I don't see them until the next day. What do I do?"*

From now on, don't think of holidays as existing on only one day; you can move any holiday on the calendar. You can move birthdays, Christmas Day, Mother's Day, Father's Day, Easter, and *any holiday* that is special to your family. The actual day does not matter, it's how you treat your family members and celebrate the event that really counts.

Negotiate with your ex-spouse on an agreement of holidays. Most common agreements work around an even/odd years approach. That way, you know years in advance what holidays the children will be with you in your home. You will also prevent many arguments if you agree upon this before any major holidays and just stick to your written agreement. A rotating system is fair for all.

### Make it fun
Children are confused when they realize they will celebrate the same holiday at mom's house and then a few days later at dad's house. Resist the temptation to celebrate together. Children harbor hopes that their parents will reunite someday. Celebrating together, as a couple, misleads your children, if you have no intention of reconciling.

Talk with your kids about the opportunity to celebrate a holiday more than once. Remind them that they will get to: eat more cookies, open more gifts and have more fun, as they rotate between the houses.

### Question:
*"My children want to spend their birthdays alone with me. I value that one on one time. My new spouse usually celebrates birthdays as a family. What should we do?"*

One-on-one time is crucial to have with each of your children. (Those of you with more than 3 children—I admire you and wish you the best!!) However, it is important to use each holiday to demonstrate to your kids that you are now a blended family; with a new stepparent and the stepsiblings.

Take birthdays as an opportunity to celebrate together, as a family. Have all members of the family bring a gift. Even little ones can make a hand made gift to give. Have a meal, serve a cake, sing "Happy Birthday," open gifts, and honor the birthday boy/girl with this family event. Mom can take the birthday child out later for an afternoon or morning outing—just the two of them, but this should not preclude the family birthday celebration.

## Celebrating the differences

### Question:
*"Our children are so different and each family has celebrated the holidays in many different ways. How should we handle the differences?"*

Being different is not so bad. If everyone were the same, your holidays would be pretty boring. Talk with each child about what makes the holidays special for him or her. Ask about foods, games, and stories that make the holidays special.

You can incorporate traditions from your previous family if they send a message of love and warmth to your child. Examples may include attending a Christmas Eve service, reading Christmas stories, or visiting special holiday lights shows.

Make sure you include equal amounts of traditions from both sides of your blended family. Have the child who requested the event explain it to the others in the family. Make sure everyone participates in each event.

## Holiday meals
Create the holiday meal as a compilation of all of the children's requests. Ask relatives for recipes, if the requested dish is one in which you are not

familiar. Each holiday meal should have some sense of familiarity for each child.

Create a fun meal the second night of the holidays. Ordering pizza is easy or something more unusual such cooking by the fire in the backyard, making their favorite appetizers, or eating breakfast for dinner.

## Birthdays

Ask the birthday boy or girl what they would like to eat. Let the birthday child choose their meal. All blended family members should be present and participate in the celebration.

### Bonus Idea

Visit one of the local pottery businesses and create your own "You are Special" plate. Decorate it with red hearts or bright colors. On a family member's birthday or any special occasion (high grades, winning a sports event or receiving an award,) the honored child gets to eat off the "You are Special" plate.

## Decorating the house for the holidays

Make sure all children are home when you decorate for the holidays. Give each child an assignment or section of the house to decorate. This is a great time to allow each child to invite a friend over, have holiday music playing, and pizza and snacks in the kitchen. Let each child choose some of the music and rotate the choices throughout the day.

Assign areas of the house, and put the allotted decorations in this area. Give each child and her team a lot of freedom to decorate. Provide some guidance, but give them the opportunity to express their own creativity with the decorations.

Make this a fun day, and one they will remember as a positive day with their blended family. If you are able to combine siblings and stepsiblings in a project, this is even better, but do not worry about pushing this. The stepsiblings may not be interacting much, but they are working together on a united purpose, decorating their home. Your house and tree may not look as perfect as if you decorated it all yourself, but your children and stepchildren will have a sense of ownership since they had an active part in the decorating process.

For your Christmas tree, use ornaments from both family's trees. If you can, put photos of each child on the tree (mounting the ornaments at eye level is best.) If you have ornaments that the children have made in their early childhood, also put these items on the tree. Make sure each child sees familiar ornaments on the tree. Make sure that there are an equal number of ornaments of each child on the tree (yes, the children will count them.)

When shopping as a family, choose some new ornaments to put on your tree. You are building your new traditions with the new ornaments. This is also a time to celebrate your marriage and have photo ornaments of you and your spouse. You can also purchase special ornaments to commemorate your marriage, first Christmas, or new house. These ornaments celebrate your life and your new marriage.

If you have younger children, ages 3-11, let them have their own children's tree. This is an additional tree that they are allowed to decorate with ornaments of their choice, and redecorate (take the ornaments on and off the tree repeatedly) throughout the holidays. These ornaments may be of cartoon characters, or all handmade, or any assortment of kid-themed items. Use ornaments on strings, without the metal hooks for the safety of the younger ones.

**Bonus Idea:**
Purchase personalized ornaments and put each child's name on each ornament. If there is an ornament that requires a family name, label it "Our Family" since stepsiblings usually have a different last name.

**What about the gifts?**
It is important that you are equal in every sense: number of gifts, total cost, everything!! Are the children watching? You bet they are. They are counting gift boxes, seeing if any child is favored. This is an important time to teach your children that each one of them is special and an important part of your blended family. All children should be treated equally at Christmas, birthdays, or any other holiday you celebrate. Make a note to spend the same amount on each child at each event. If varying ages make this difficult, still try to keep celebrations and gifts as even as possible.

It is also important to exchange gifts between the children. Spending a great deal of money is not important. It will be easy for each child to find a gift for their biological sibling, but it is important for them to try to get to know their new stepsibling, and choose a gift for them. (Dollar store gifts are fine, or handmade gifts, if money is tight, as long as everyone spends the same amount on gifts.) It's the thought that counts, not the money spent.

Guide children to purchase a gift for their new stepparent. This is important and shows respect for the new relationship. Again, the amount of money spent does not matter, as long as all gifts from children to stepparents are equal. A spreadsheet may be helpful in figuring all this out.

### Other Questions:
*"What happens with the gifts they receive from their other parent? How can we keep this fair?"*

You really cannot keep the gifts coming from other biological parents equal and fair. What you can do is encourage children to not talk about these gifts outside of the home in which the gifts are given. Encourage children to be considerate of their new blended family and treat each stepsibling the way they would want to be treated.

*"What about gifts from extended family members?"*

Encourage grandparents, aunts and uncles to acknowledge the new stepchildren and honor them equally with gifts. If this means that all receive less expensive gifts, that is better than sending gifts to the "real grandchildren" and ignoring the new step grandchildren. Set an example to extended family by embracing your new blended family, and talking about your expectations to relatives. Explain to your extended family that you are treating everyone equally and would like for them to accept your entire blended family in their holiday celebrations and gift exchanges.

### Bonus Idea:
Send out Christmas cards with your blended family photograph on it. "From Our Family to Yours" is a great way to express your desire to introduce your blended family to extended relatives and friends.

## How to talk to extended family about the holidays
This is a new experience for your own Mom or Dad, and other extended family members. Talk with them about how you want to create an inclusive

relationship with all of your family members. Explain how you are treating all children equally and how you would expect them to do the same with your children and new stepchildren.

Give extended family members ideas on gifts, since they may not know your new family members as well. Clearly explain that the monetary amount of each gift is not what is important, but acknowledging all family members equally is crucial.

Include extended family members in some of your holiday events. Spend time talking with your spouse about what events you want to include extended family members in, and what events you want only you and all of your kids involved. Your new blended family needs to have a feeling that they are a new unit, and sometimes events are so special that only they are invited.

Outings with your children that exclude the stepsiblings are O.K., as long as they are not very long or are very special events. Splitting up to run errands is fine, but spending the day in a theme park, while the stepsiblings stay at home is not. Remember at all times to treat your stepchildren the way you want your children to be treated.

**School plays and other special holiday and school events**
Special school events and other holiday events are important to your child and to your blended family. If possible, attend a child's school event with all family members present. This shows the child that their stepsiblings and their new stepparent support them. Make sure you actively participate and pay attention to the school event. If you're the photographer in the family, don't forget to take photos! After the event, talk with your stepchild and ask questions about the event. Make sure you show a genuine interest in your stepchild and her event.

You and your spouse should also attend all of these events together. You should be seen as a couple and the center of this new marriage. Sitting with your ex-spouse is O.K., as long as you have your new spouse with you. Taking photos to celebrate the event, together with your ex-spouse in the photo, is not acceptable. This creates unrealistic expectations of your child, who may be secretly hoping her parents will be getting back together.

Always allow your children and stepchildren to see you and your spouse as a unit. If you disagree about how to handle events—talk with your spouse in private. Once you agree, present a united front to the children and stepchildren when you discuss your decision.

### Question:
*"My child feels threatened by my new spouse at school events. He wants me to attend the event, but not my spouse, what should I do?"*

Explain to your child that you love him and will always be his parent. Remarrying does not change your relationship. Discuss how this new stepparent is an additional person to support and love him, but does not take away from the love of his real mom and dad. Also, summarize that this is your new spouse, who you love very much, and you appreciate their interest in your children and their willingness to attend the events. Stress that you will be attending as a married couple to their events, so that both of you can support your child.

**Family photos: scrapbook albums, holiday cards and group photos**
Depending on how long you have been married, it might not be a good time to put everyone in the car and drive down to your local portrait studio for a family photo. It is important for your children and stepchildren to see you as one new unit, but you pushing them into a formal group photo, so that you can send out a Christmas card as one, big, happy family, is a little unrealistic.

Take candid shots of your children and stepchildren during the holidays. Create a photo album or scrapbook to chronicle these important family events. If you have a shot with stepsiblings together, take it, and be happy that the stepsiblings are getting to know each other.

Each family event will become easier. As you and your spouse set the example that you are enjoying time with all of your children together, this shows your children that it is O.K. to have fun with their new stepsiblings. Remember, you have gotten to know your spouse during the dating and courtship period, so now provide fun opportunities for your children to get to know their stepsiblings.

**Note:** the time for taking photos of you and your children, without your new spouse or stepsiblings in the picture, is over. Any photos like this will increase divisiveness in the home. Think of your family as a whole, not two units put together.

## Creating traditions for your blended family

As you talk with each child about what is special to them about the holidays, it is time to develop traditions of your own. Create a special meal that everyone in your family participates. This meal could be making pizzas, preparing their favorite appetizers, or a theme night (i.e. Mexican food, Chinese food, picnic food.)

Making stockings with each child's name on it is a wonderful tradition. Inexpensive stockings are readily available for you to cut and iron-on each child's name. We label the parent stockings "Mom" and "Dad" on one side, and "Shirley" and "Eric" on the other side. (This keeps both our biological children and stepchildren happy.) Fill the stockings with fun items and special treats. Remember, equality is everything. As your child opens his stocking, he is also peaking at the stocking of his new stepsibling. As you purchase stocking treats, maintain equality at all costs. Seeing their stockings lined up by the fireplace, or under the tree, again shows that you are one family, ready to celebrate the season.

Purchase a wreath and choose the decorations together. A brand new wreath on the door symbolizes your new family.

### Bonus Ideas:

Fall is a great season to create traditions. Purchase pumpkins and carve them together. Younger kids can paint their pumpkins. Have fun music and snacks available as the new stepsiblings work on their pumpkins.

Easter is a time for small children to enjoy Easter egg hunts. Have older siblings and stepsiblings hide the eggs and treats. This will allow all ages to participate in the hunt together.

## Couple time during the holidays

Don't forget during the holidays that you are married to a wonderful person. This person is someone you chose to change your life, move in together and join your families. Couple time is very important, but often forgotten. You and your spouse should have a dedicated time several times a month. Schedule more time if possible. This is your time, to spend some quality time with each other, and children are not invited. The holidays are so busy, you may want to skip your couple time, but as the busyness and stresses of the holiday increase, finding time for your spouse should become more important.

Ideally, it's great to have couple time each evening. This is a time for you and your spouse to discuss the day, cover any areas you would like to handle differently, and just enjoy each other. You can also use this time to make decisions on future family activities or events without having your children intervene. Tell your children that this is your time, and they are not to disturb you during your couple's time.

You and your spouse are the center of the marriage, the leaders in your family. You must keep this bond strong to guide your children and stepchildren positively through life. Do not keep secrets from your spouse (that you share with your children.) These secrets put your children into the center of the marriage and this is not healthy.

**Organizing travel arrangements for your kids during the holidays**
School has started back, and the kids are on a regular schedule again—thank goodness! Now you can stop worrying about the summer visitation schedule, and long visits to the noncustodial parent. It's time to enjoy your blended family and fall back into a regular schedule.
Stop!

I wish you could relax, but it's time to plan for the holidays! Have you ever sat down, the week before Thanksgiving, and figured out no one talked about visitation? You don't know who's staying with whom, or how many are coming for the Thanksgiving meal? It's just crazy to not plan ahead!

### Coordinating the schedules
Planning your calendar makes life easier for everyone. If you've remarried, and your ex-spouse has remarried, (and the people they remarried were married before) your schedule can effect many different families! Your children also need to know where they will be, on different weekends, so they can also make plans.

I hope that you have already determined the holiday visitation schedule, when you completed a separation agreement. If not—common agreements include that the dad will have the kids over Christmas on even ending years, and the mom will have them on odd ending years. Children transition to the other home Christmas afternoon, evening, or the next day. Other holidays are decided the same (with the even/odd year schedule.) Example: If dad has the kids on the even ending years, then he will have them on the odd ending years during Thanksgiving and Spring break.

## Mode of transportation

So—check your calendar and start figuring out how to transport your child to your ex's house. Will they travel by car, train, or airplane? Amtrak and the airlines provide special services for the unaccompanied child, but you must state that your child is traveling alone, when you make the reservation. Reservations made earlier will get you a better rate than waiting until weeks before your child's visit.

Communicate with your ex-spouse before making any final arrangements. Make sure you give them at least several weeks (to talk with the other families) to confirm the dates and travel plans.

## Getting your child organized

It's helpful to give your child his or her own personal calendar, with the visitation dates clearly marked. Having a large calendar in the kitchen, with each child a different color, will also help coordinate your family. If your child knows their schedule, it will give her a sense of continuity and stability. They can look at their own calendar anytime they are unsure about when the next visit to mom or dad's house will be.

## Clothes

Start marking their clothes if your child is visiting a house with other children that are the same size and gender. Marking their initials on the insides of clothing will mean your child comes home with his or her own clothes and not the wardrobe of a child that's not yours! We've had a child come home with size 3 Batman underwear (he's 17 and as big as an adult!) and also "lose" half his blue jeans, over the holidays. Mark their initials on all the clothes. It's also helpful to include a list of all clothes that are being sent. If the noncustodial parent (or their spouse) does laundry, they will have a checklist to make sure everything goes back home.

Does everything still fit? Children grow constantly, and you don't want to send your child to a noncustodial parent's house with clothes or shoes that are too short or small. Does your child have enough underwear and socks for a week without laundry? You may want to discuss with your ex-spouse if your child's clothes can be washed during their visit.

## Proper luggage

Check your child's luggage. Are their any tears or damage to the luggage that will not be good for travel? Children may not mention little holes in luggage, but with the ruggedness of travel, you can lose a lot of precious valuables through a little hole! Follow the sales in the local papers, and you can pick up a large set of luggage inexpensively. Make sure you also purchase luggage tags, so that your child's name and address is marked on each piece of his luggage.

## Medicine and vitamins

Do you need medicine containers to transport medicine? Make sure you also send instructions to the noncustodial parent, on how to administer the medicine. It's best to send medicine in its original containers. Also, talk with your child about being responsible for taking their vitamins and medicine daily. If you plan ahead and stay organized, the scheduling of your child's holiday visitation will go more smoothly.

### Question
*"I have a child that just does not want to "blend." She pouts, has temper tantrums, and refuses to participate in our blended family events. What should we do?"*

Some children take longer than others to accept change. Some are less emotionally developed than others (age does not have anything to do with emotional development.) Continue to tell your child that you love her and the relationship with her has not changed. You have added family members to her life to love and support her. Encourage her to participate in family events but also allow her to sit, a little apart, and watch, if she does not feel comfortable joining in. Do not give her extra attention; just continue enjoying your family event, showing her that you are having fun.

Do not allow any disrespectful behavior or rudeness to a new stepparent or stepsiblings. Any negative action requires immediate discipline and removing the child from the activity; taking away any additional privileges. If any rudeness or disrespectfulness occurs, leave the child at home alone (if old enough) or with another adult (if younger) and proceed with the activity. Make sure the child does not feel rewarded, but feels left out of the event. Take away additional privileges or future opportunities until your child understands that this negative behavior is not acceptable. Do not devote much time to this, but move forward with your family events.

### Question
*"My child keeps bringing up "the old days" and wants to talk about how things used to be? How can I bring my child into reality and the present without disparaging the past?"*

Spend time talking with your child about how you love them and also have fond memories of the past. Tell them that, although you too have good memories, you are no longer married to their other parent. Explain that the reasons for divorce are very complicated, and although you can discuss it briefly, it is something that they are not going to completely understand, or need to understand.

Tell them that you have remarried and are very happy. Discuss your new family and how it makes you proud to see all of them together. Tell your child that you are moving forward, positively, with your new blended family, and making new memories to remember. Ask your child to be a part of these new traditions and memories.

# House Hunting for the Blended Family

**Budget**

Discuss with your future spouse the ideal budget for a new home. Make sure you choose a range that you can afford. Try to keep your house payments to 25% of your income (33% at the very most.) You may have two houses that need selling. Make sure at least one of the houses is sold before you purchase another home.

**Agree on the area of town**

- Are you trying to stay in a certain school district?
- Will the new house be relatively (but not too close) to your ex-spouse's house? This makes dropping off and picking up children easier.

**Involve the kids in the house hunting process**

Ask children what's most important to have in their new home. You may be surprised at how helpful their answers will be. Allow your kids to come on selected trips with the realtor. The best times to involve the kids are in the beginning, when you are only driving around looking, and in the end (when you have found a house you believe will work, and want them to tour it with you.)

**Bathrooms**

- It's important to have separate bathrooms, if possible, for the boys and the girls. Adequate bathrooms are actually more important than the number of bedrooms.
- Make sure you and your spouse have your own bathroom, separate from the kids.

## Bedrooms

- It's not as important for each child to have his own bedroom. Children that visit, but don't live in the house full-time, can share a bedroom.
- If you use a pullout couch or basement room for the visiting child, make sure they have enough privacy and that they can keep personal items in this area.
- Give children the opportunity to make decisions about their rooms, such as paint color, curtains and comforters.

## Living Spaces

- If your kids are varied in ages, it's helpful to have several places "to be" in the house for entertaining, watching T.V., and just hanging out. Consider a house with a basement or with several floors, so that your kids can spread out and find their own space to relax.
- Look for privacy in the master bedroom. It's helpful to find a house that has the master bedroom sectioned off from the other bedrooms, if possible. You and your new spouse need your own space, too.

## Final Tips:

Remember, you and your spouse are the center of the family, the core of the relationship. Input from all of your blended family is helpful, but ultimately you and your spouse make the final decisions on what house you purchase. This carefully selected house will become the home for your new blended family.

## Good luck house hunting!

# Special Report: Golden Rules for Grandparents in a Blended Family

You and your new spouse have had some time, getting to know each other, and deciding to blend your families. Even though you are adults, hopefully you introduced your new love to your parents before the wedding. After the wedding, it's time to help your mom and dad with some tips on how to respond to your newly blended family.

## 1—Treat all children equally and fairly

Treat your step grandkids as if they were all your biological grandchildren. They are waiting and watching to see if you will be fair to all. If your biological grandchildren call you "grandmother"—then invite your new step grandchildren to call you "grandmother." If you hug your grandchildren when you see them, and then hug your step grandchildren, too.

Dispense with the "biological" and "step" labels as soon as you can. Even keeping these labels in your head may cause you to treat your grandchildren unequally.

## 2—Express interest in each child

Make time to learn about your new step grandchildren: their activities, friends and hobbies. Figure out what makes each child unique. These endeavors will help you feel more comfortable around them, and help you get to know them.

### 3—Remember special days

Acknowledge birthdays, school events, and any other special activities of your new step grandkids. At the beginning of each year, mark all special events on the calendar. You may even want to purchase birthday cards or gift cards—all at once. That way you are fair to all and don't forget anyone.

Don't forget your new daughter or son in law, too. Remembering them with a card on their birthday will help show your support for the marriage. Share information about your family history or family recipes, to help your daughter or son (by marriage) feel a part of your family.

### 4—Don't reminisce about the past

Your adult child has divorced and moved on to a new marriage. Recalling the good times in their old marriage is not going to help with blending the new marriage. Take the old wedding photos off the wall and put them away in a special album. It's O.K. to keep these pictures, but do not display the old marriage partners on the wall for everyone to see when they visit you.

### 5—Listen

When your adult child calls and wants to talk about their frustrating moments in their blended family, but don't judge or say anything negative that you'll regret later. It's very difficult to blend a family and requires a lot of patience. Support your son or daughter as they try their best to be a good parent and spouse in this new blended family.

**In conclusion**—remember it's your job to love all of your grandchildren and support your adult child and his/her spouse in their new blended family. It's a little new and unfamiliar at first, but well worth your efforts. You will have the reward of a bigger family to love you back.

Thank you for loving and supporting your adult child in his or her new blended family. Your new daughter or son in-law will appreciate your efforts more than you will ever know. You new step-grandchildren will love you as their own grand parent. There really isn't any negative aspects to loving your new blended family as your own. Thank you for your flexibility and love.

# Notes

_____

_____

_____

_____

_____

_____

_____

_____

_____

_____

_____

_____

_____

_____

_____

_____

_____

_____

_____

_____

_____

_____

**Contact Us:**
We would love you hear your family's experiences, comments and questions after reading *Blended Family Advice*, along with the bonus reports.

Contact us at The Blended and Step Family Resource Center:
Shirley@blendedfamilyadvice.com

For additional resources, ebooks, and newsletters, visit our website at:
www.BlendedFamilyAdvice.com
www.TheBlendedandStepFamilyResourceCenter.com